The Online MARKETING BLUEPRINT

How To Create An Online Strategy That Works For You

Including A Proven Step By Step Framework

Author: Thierry Moubax

Blue Compass Press
The Online Marketing Blueprint –
How to create an Online Strategy that Works for You
Thierry Moubax

Copyeditor: Kirkus Media
Cover Design & Formatting: Anita Jovanovic
Illustrations: Alexander Pokusay

If you would like to do any of the above, please seek permission first by contacting us at www.bluecompass.eu or www.braintower.com

Published in Belgium by Blue Compass Press

ISBN: 9789082279610

Dedicated

To my wife, Felisa and my two kids, Guillermo and Sofia.
You give me so much joy and the energy of life.

To my Dad, we lost you too soon.
You gave me my unlimited desire to learn and read.

Contents

"Being rich is not about how much money you have or how many homes you own;
It's the freedom to buy any book you want
Without looking at the price and wondering if you can afford it."

John Waters

Introduction

If you are reading this page you've probably tried to start an online channel or at least are thinking about it, but are frustrated that it is not so easy or that it doesn't give the desired result. You feel there's opportunity, but just don't know how or what to do to exploit it.

The world has changed dramatically over the last decade. The Internet has been around since the early nineties, but it is only recently that we have seen exponential online growth. There are now over two billion users online and this number will increase dramatically when all the developing countries join. And this is ready to become a reality because six billion people own mobile phones. There are more people with a mobile phone than who have access to a toilet! People everywhere, and anywhere, are continually connected to the outside world. As the number of individuals with cell phones and on the Internet grows, so does the potential pool of website users. Facebook, of course, is a prime example. This social website now has more users than the entire Internet had a decade ago.

Businesses used to have a certain degree of control over their customers. At least they decided what to inform them. People used to listen to the sales people as the main information-gathering channel. Today the customer can get all the information they want and more: the basic product information, professional reviews, reviews from users, or ask their five-hundred-plus friends on Facebook for their opinion. In many cases, a potential buyer is probably more educated than the sales person. This new customer does not go to the shop to get information, but rather to experience the product: to touch, feel, sense, or smell it, or just to have a nice moment. If your product or service does not need this live experience before purchase the likelihood that your need to have a shop is becoming less important.

You have no "control" over classic communication channels. With the quantity of information produced and ads that we are exposed to continuously, the new customer has developed better filters to survive this tsunami of information. The filters are very sophisticated and are like radar that detects non-interesting stuff to ignore. Do the following exercise: Try remembering the hundreds of ads you have been exposed to today. Do you understand the filters we have? This capability of filtering is not even a luxury anymore. We live in a world of "dis-traction!" The next time you are in a meeting room look around you and watch the "focused" people who check every five minutes to see if new e-mail has popped into their mailbox. We watch a second screen—smartphone or tablet—while watching television, but we still expect the traditional TV ads to be as effective as they were ten years ago.

A well designed and optimized website could have worked in the past but today, without a good digital strategy, companies quickly fall behind or completely loose the race. It's not about spending more on technology or improving your site. If your site is like a beautiful mall in the desert, you'll have a hard time if there are no roads that head its way.

Another big transformation is the way that the customer has changed from being a reactive information consumer to an information creator. And think of content in a broad context: blogs, tweets, status updates on Facebook, comments and ratings of the products purchased, books read, apps played with, or experiences in hotels. And if we also take into consideration all the shares and the likes on the content consumed the growth is even more spectacular.

In the "old world," a decade ago, we knew who our competitors were. Today "small" companies or individuals from all around the globe are competing with established corporations. Billion-dollar companies such as Kodak, Blockbuster, and Borders have gone bankrupt because they were not able to see and adapt to these changes, while small start-ups have had exponential growth. Google, for example, acquired YouTube, for $1.6 billion after it had been around for only eighteen months.

The former logic that a company had to grow in size to achieve economies of scale is obsolete. The new digital platforms make scaling possible without really growing in size. New online entrants exploit existing platforms; they don't have to create them. They do it at a lower cost with faster speed of implementation. Some offer their products for free and monetize only when they have reached a massive user base. The mere fact that established companies resist the changes just allows the new disruptors to have it easier. The security and confidence that existed in the past and that we were taught from childhood does not belong in our vocabulary anymore. Companies to work for over a lifetime, or lifetime state jobs . . . More Fortune 500 companies will disappear if they are not able to cope with these changes. Technology is radically changing the world and altering our "secure foundations." The only security that exists today is that there is and will be CONSTANT CHANGE. We think linear, but technological growth is exponential.

So how do we keep on track or take advantage of these changes?

Most people will see this as a big problem and try to firefight the changes; because humans are motivated to prevent the loss of what they have today. This is psychologically wired in us, so the great majority fears these changes. But where there is a problem, people look for solutions, because the problem has to be solved! And as Winston Churchill said, "A pessimist sees difficulties in every opportunity and an optimist sees opportunities in every difficulty." Never has there been a better time than now to start a new business. Just look at young people like Mark Zuckerberg who have become millionaires or billionaires. You might think Zuckerberg is an exception, and indeed there are not so many new billionaires, but you would be surprised how many young "anonymous kids" become millionaires these days using the online world without any previous business experience in the off-line world or no entrepreneurial experience at all.

However I don't want to give you a false impression that it's easy, and when you knock on the door of opportunity people are surprised that the answer is work. But how to fulfill the work has changed. Today you don't need to be a geek or technological savvy nor spend huge amounts of money to start an online business. You cannot see technology as a bottleneck or problem anymore but you have to see it as an enabler. You just need to be the architect and know what is possible and which tools to use.

I've been working in the corporate world for almost twenty years and I was watching the online evolution and the digital disruption from this side and was frustrated about it. Not because I was relying on external agencies to do our online campaigns, but rather because I felt deep inside that I could also play a role in this online space. I was leaving big opportunities on the table. I liked the topic but did not really know how to start and what to do. I was watching a game without being able to play it, but knowing that I was able to. Had I known what I know today, I might have been one of those young kids, too.

So I started reading dozens, hundreds of books on the topic, I bought very expensive courses, and started going to seminars even to the United States. My wife thought I was crazy to spend forty hours traveling for three or four days of seminars—don't even mention the money or the jetlag. But I was determined to master the online marketing subjects and implement them. Because learning the theory is one thing, and I still see so many "academic" talks of people who haven't walked the walk. So in 2010 I decided to quit the corporate world and get into the trenches and start my own business. I took two very successful Internet marketers that I met at a seminar in San Diego as mentors, Trey Smith[1] and Ed Dale[2] and started an app business. I started to create educational apps for kids between three and eight years. When my kids where young I had always wanted to create flash games to help them learning to read or count. With my passion for education and the iPad booming, I was convinced that I could be a part of that revolution. It was not always easy but I had a desire to succeed. I am neither a developer nor a designer, but with today's global access, I knew I could find good professionals to help me with this project. After some trial and error I found some good guys and started my online journey. Not all the money I invested was a success. I failed with several of my apps. In fact the most expensive one to realize, a puzzle game to learn animals has been a big flop. Because

---

1   Trey Smith is an Internet marketer from San Diego, founder of GameAcademy. com and very successful App builder.

2   Ed Dale is a successful Australian Internet marketer.

I did not do the proper pre-analysis, my launch was not good and I did not apply the growth hacking strategy: finding out what the user wants – something I'll explain later. But I learned from my failures and improved the apps and marketing behind them, and after six months, I already had a profitable app.

In the initial phase my business model was only based on premium apps or better known as paid apps. Then I added a *freemium* model, which means you get a part for free, and if you want more—you pay, and added some apps with advertising and others with in-app purchases.

Now I've reached the point where I have a continuous download rate of more than two thousand apps per day, without having to spend much on advertising in it. More than one million kids from all over the globe have already downloaded and played with my apps. I can assure you that this feeling of excitement was something I had not felt while I was in the corporate life. I had created a stable income that many would dream of. However it's not the money that gave me the biggest kick; one of the nicest rewards has been a comment from a mother of a Down syndrome child who asked me if she could have some promotional codes to promote my apps in her charity foundation. She saw good progress in the learning process of her child and wanted to help other kids with it. For clarity, I am not a professional educator; I'm just the father of two kids and I like the topic of education. But now that I've achieved this, I'm convinced that everyone can do it, whether you are starting up a company, or have an established small or medium company, or are working for a Fortune 500. Mastering online marketing will bring you to other levels.

And this is the reason I wrote this book: I want to continue my education, but it is not about teaching kids to learn or to count, even if it is very exciting. Instead it's about wanting to share my insights with marketers and business people around the globe. Today I'm helping start-ups, small and medium enterprises (SMEs), corporations, and governmental institutions with their marketing strategy both on- and off-line. My objective with this book is to help you, too, so that you can take advantage of the opportunities.

The key factor to success in business is knowing how to sell and market a product, but the way to do so has completely changed in the last years. You don't have to be an expert in the whole field of digital marketing to be successful online, but you should know some of the basics as: defining and analyzing your target audience and competition; the types of traffic, how to set up an online sales funnel and why and how to use social media. This is what this book is all about. Most seminars, webinars, or courses on Internet marketing cover just one subject and support this with case studies from a year or two ago. One seminar will cover social media, another stresses apps, a third talks about new forms of digital content—e-books, e-zines, and downloadable white papers. To connect all the dots, you need to go to a lot of seminars and read a lot of books.

But you will not have to spend countless hours and money as I did, this book will be your shortcut and it will be your guide to understand and develop a successful online marketing strategy. As Brendon Burchard, says *"The best time to have the map is before you enter the wood."*[3]

And don't think that you will only get the basics; I'll go into depth, enough so that you will feel confident and will be able to take advantage of these opportunities.

- You will discover the important changes that affect your business.
- You'll learn what has changed in marketing and sales and how to adapt to it
- And you'll find out what you should and should not do.

I'll give you a framework that explains step-by-step WHAT and HOW to set up your online marketing. Even if you have never done it before or if you're not yet part of the Facebook community or not Tweeting, after reading this book you should know more than 99% of your peers. Be open-minded. The only ingredient that you need is the desire to learn and implement what you learn. But if you read this book and do not take action, do not complain afterwards that the world is

3   Brendon Burchard is a #1 *New York Times* bestselling author of *The Millionaire Messenger,* and the The *Charge: Activating the 10 Human Drives That Make You Feel Alive.*

changing and your business is decreasing because of unfair competition. I've also procrastinated during many years and now I realize that I've lost all that time. The most successful business people are those who take action. It won't be perfect from scratch. It never is. But if you fear to fall you'll never learn to walk, let alone run a marathon!

Therefore I really hope my book will inspire you to take these first steps into a new direction and that it will help you and be your guide to a new way of doing Marketing.

I invite you to share with me your reactions to this book

Thierry Moubax

For individuals: moubax@bluecompass.eu
For companies: Thierry.moubax@braintower.com
Or follow me on Facebook: https://www.facebook.com/moubax or
LinkedIn: be.linkedin.com/in/moubax

I've structured the book in three parts:

Part 1 is an introduction to the new disruptive world. I'll explain the digital changes and why and how the new connected customer and the new competition affect your business model.

In **Part 2**, I'll cover how things have changed in sales and marketing. I'll also explain what I call the Ten Marketing Myths—how marketing used to be in the past but does not work anymore today, and what you really should do about it to be successful.

Part 3 is the core of this book. Here I will give you a step-by-step framework of what you have to do.

- **The ABC foundation** to start with before you go to Market
- **The Six-step sales funnel**
- **The leverage phase**: how to get your clients to come back and help you find more customers.

It continues with Marketing Automation. Speed of implementation is crucial these days, so finding ways to automate and increase your marketing is crucial. This will enable you to grow your business quickly, but more importantly it will allow you to scale without extra sales resources

This model can be used in many industries regardless of the size of the company, and it will allow you to better identify, acquire, and grow customers.

PART 1

The New Digital World

*"Change is the law of life.
And those who look only to the past or present
are certain to miss the future"*

John F. Kennedy

When Tim Berners-Lee invented the World Wide Web, I doubt that he realized the impact that it would have on humanity—how it would radically change the way we live, the way we communicate, and the way we do business. Today over two billion people[4] are connected to the Internet and most forecasts predict that this number will double in the coming years. I still remember in 1994, when I worked for Shell, we were

---

4   Internet world stats reported mid 2014 that there were 2,405,518,376 people
    connected to the Internet (http://www.internetworldstats.com)

"going on the Internet" in the computer room. This was still a luxury for the happy few. The accessibility increased with the democratization of the laptop and Internet access prices, but it was not until the introduction of the smartphones, BlackBerries, iPhones, and Android devices that we saw the big breakthrough in connectivity. Today, according to the International Telecommunication Union[5], there are 7 billion mobile cellular subscriptions on earth. We have nearly reached the point of full penetration, meaning that everyone has a mobile phone on earth!

Many of these devices are "smart," meaning connectable to the Internet. Globally, mobile-broadband penetration will reach 32% by end 2014, 2,4 billion, almost double the penetration rate of just three years before (2011), and four times higher than five years ago (2009).

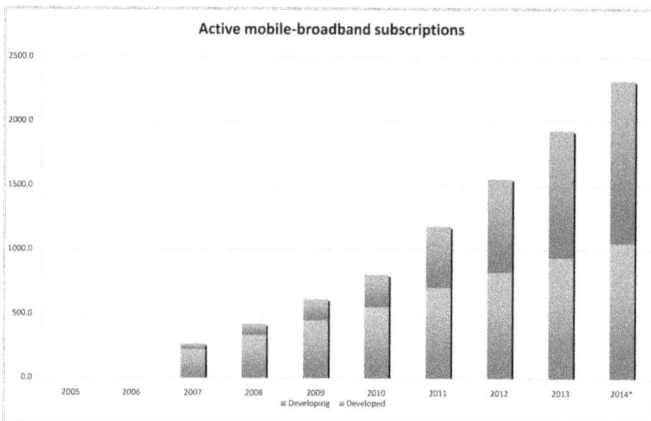

Illustration 1.1: Active Mobile-broadband subscriptions, source ITU

It's not a surprise that the mobile phone has seen such a quick development and penetration. We have always been mobile creatures who are "on the move." It is only in the last fifty years that we have started a sedentary life and working at a desk and that back pain has emerged. A mobile device is now like a third arm; it is the first thing we look at in the morning and the last thing before we go to sleep.

---

5   ITU is the United Nation Specialized agency

And when these mobiles became smart the impact became gigantic. Today, a poor resident of Namibia with a smartphone has access to more information than the president of the United States did fifteen years ago.

In just one generation, we have gained access to all kinds of unfiltered information. We can get information on everything we want and solve problems through a simple Google search, and even more if we include the recent Wikileaks and Snowden affairs. What paradoxically was a luxury twenty years ago—being able to speak with someone via "mobile"—today has been flipped on its side; being without a mobile phone even for a couple of hours is considered a near impossibility. So, most of the planet has the potential of using the Internet with immediate access to all of its available information.

And this is just the beginning: When the rest of the planet, or the nearly six other billion people come online, there will be a new Internet revolution. But there is even more . . . Not only humans are connected to the Internet. Besides the three billion smartphones, laptops, or desktop computers, there are many other devices that are connected online. This is what is typically known as the Internet of Things. You might think of products like wearables. These are miniature electronic devices that are worn by the users that have constant interaction between the computer and user. They often include tracking information related to health and fitness. Some examples are Fitbit or Pebble. Other better-known wearable are the Google Glass and the Apple Watch, Apple's first real wearable. All these devices are still seen as gadgets and may account to only a small fraction of what the Internet of Things will be. We are only at the start of this new revolution. The illustration 1.2 on The Internet of Everything is a prediction of the growth we might see in the coming years.

The Internet Of Everything

Number Of Devices In Use Globally (In Thousands)

Connected Cars

Wearables

Connected TVs

Internet Of Things

Tablets

Smartphones

PCs

Source: BI Intelligence Estimates

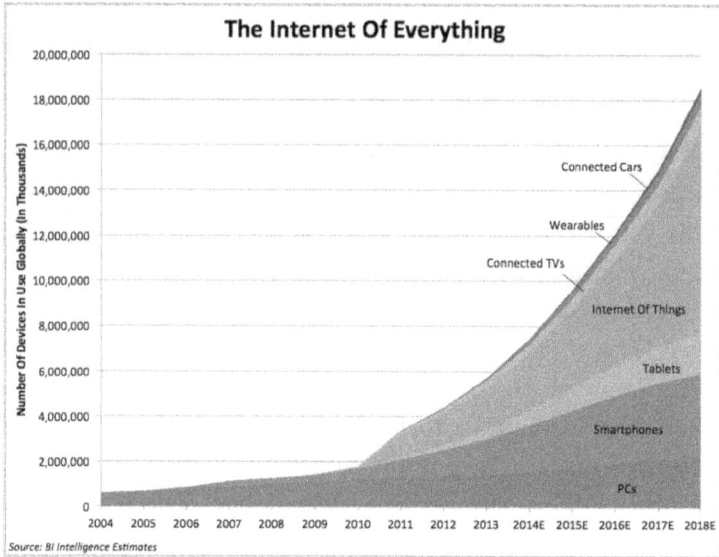

Illustration 1.2 : The Internet of Everything[6]

Morgan Stanley forecasts that by 2020 eighty billion devices will be connected to the Internet[7]. We already have a lot of automation in our cars without knowing this, and some of them are already connected to the Interet. Google has already been testing the driverless car for a couple of years in Nevada, and it is just a matter of time before these cars will be 100 percent reliable and made commercially available. As a side note: One of their objectives is to save 30,000 lives per year and to prevent another 2.2 million driver-related accidents. But the connection of things will not be limited to cars: We will see the same happen in our homes. All electronic devices might be connected to the Internet and we will be able to manage our house from a distance. Imagine all possibilities: improving security, being able to switch on or off devices

---

6   https://intelligence.businessinsider.com/the-internet-of-things-2013-10

7   Source: Morgan Stanley took Cisco's Internet of things reporting data and predicted 75 billion figure."Cisco estimates that only 200 million things were connected in 2000. Extrapolating the same growth rate up until 2020, this could mean that 75 billion things could be connected by then"

from a thousand miles away, pre-warming your oven before you arrive home, opening the door for employees only on certain days of the week, inventorying the fridge and ordering automatically! This is not science fiction anymore. The possibilities are endless. IPBuilding, a Belgian company I'm helping with their online strategy, is one of the pioneers in this field of home automation. The technology of IPBuilding enables to connect all the electric devices in a house, integrates them, and allows to communicate with them from a distance and create what we today call a smart home; improving comfort, security but also guarantees improved energy management.

We also see the growth of beacons—low-cost pieces of hardware that use Bluetooth [8] connections to deliver messages directly to a smartphone or tablet. This technology is revolutionizing the way devices can connect and interact with each other in physical spaces.

Another device that is booming is drones. These unmanned flying devices are used today mainly for military or humanitarian operations. But in the future we might see them for package deliveries, too. DHL Deutsche Post is already testing them and Amazon might use them in the future. It is unlikely that drones will be part of our lives in the immediate future, but there are many opportunities to explore for these aerial vehicles from delivering groceries to revolutionizing private security, to changing the way farmers manage their crops and maybe even aerial advertising.

We see all these new technological tools but it's not there that the biggest revolution is happening. It's not in the hardware, it's in the INFORMATION and how it is currently used or how it will be used in the future. These devices have or are enabling the massive creation of information.

The quantity of information has increased more than exponentially. Eric Schmidt, the executive chairman of Google, commented in 2010 that every two days we create as much information as we did up to 2003![9] But this data is certainly very obsolete, so we can say that 90

---

8   Bluetooth is a wireless technology standard for exchanging data over short distances

9   Eric Schmidt commented this in his presentation on 4th of Aug 2010 at the Techonomy conference in Lake Tahoe, CA

percent of all the information available has been created in the last two years. In the illustration below, an infographic that Qmee produced in 2013.[10], you can see what was been created every minute in 2013.

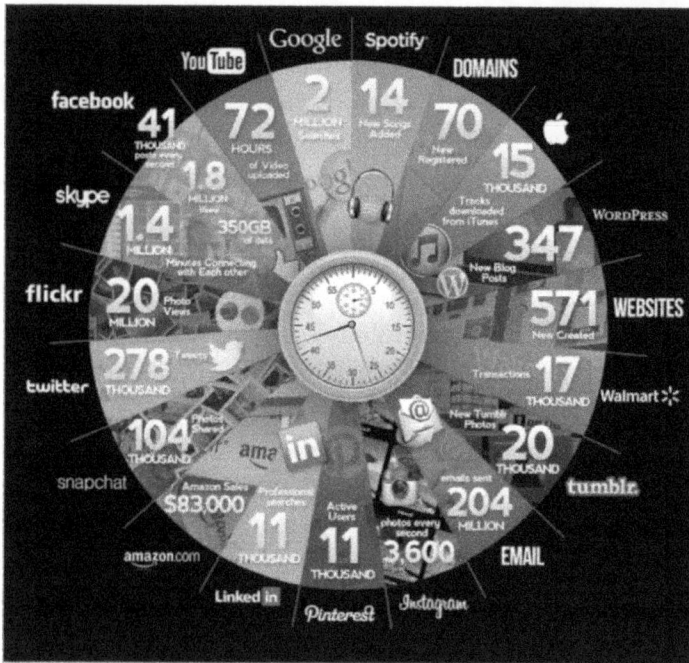

Illustration 1.3: One minute on Internet

The Internet started as a framework to consume information, then evolved into a billboard for the tech-savvy and has become THE communication platform where everyone is creating personal information and communicating to many. We take photos and produce videos and post them instantly on Facebook to share with our hundreds or thousands of friends. Ironically, perhaps we do not even talk to these so-called friends in the "real world."

And this is only what humans are producing, if you add all the potential for the Internet of Things that we will have in the future, the picture becomes daunting. Data availability and the use of it, is typically

---

10   http://blog.qmee.com/qmee-online-in-60-seconds/

called *big data*. It opens unimaginable opportunities for those that have access to it, are creative, and know how to transform it into added value. That is also the reason why you see the big brothers buying data rich companies: Facebook bought WhatsApp for $19 billion, Microsoft took over Skype for $8 billion and Google purchased Nest Labs, a company whose mission is to reinvent devices in the home such as thermostats and smoke alarms, for $3.2 billion. The future will tell us who will be the ones that best transform this raw data into valuable assets. They will have to solve the debate on privacy, but aggregated data is already opening countless opportunities.

The possibilities and changes that the availability of this information are creating is tremendous, however we, humans, still think linearly and will have difficulty keeping the same pace in our lives and businesses. Technology will not change the human DNA, at least not in the immediate future, but it has already seriously impacted the way we get what we want, and also how customers shop and buy. The customer has more information, can access this from everywhere and looks for a trusted seller in this "anonymous" virtual world to make a final purchase.

As a marketer we have to understand the underlying changes in order to set up an effective business strategy. Therefore let's take a closer look at the main parameters that have changed.

CHAPTER 1

The New Business Environment

The New Customer

The Asymmetry of Information

In the recent past, the seller had more information than the buyer. As a buyer you had to go to the seller to get this information. For example, when people wanted to purchase a car, they would go to one dealer who gave them some "filtered" information. They would then go to another dealer who told them something different. It was not easy to have a transparent view. In most cases, the buyer never knew the whole story. Today, the power of knowledge has shifted and buyers have access to the same and sometimes even more information than sellers had before. When I say more, I mean in the context of reviews and ratings. Consumers only need to go online and search for any information they want. For instance, they can easily get the latest reviews from top magazines or other customers, or a list of dealers with the lowest prices. They can easily spot the weaknesses or flaws a product might have, and with a click of a button find a competing product that is better suited to their needs.

In addition, social media sharing and consumer reviews have more influence than ever. In the past you could ask some of your friends for information, but there was no systematic way to do this in a very effortless way. Today, one posted question may trigger tens or even hundreds of answers from "trusted" friends. Apple, Google, Amazon, and many other sites use these reviews and ratings as one of the parameters of their ranking algorithms and the importance or weight of this parameter in the calculation is increasing. Look at apps or Amazons products with many ratings and consumer reviews; they typically will appear higher in the rankings. It's not the big cooks who rank a restaurant number one on sites like TripAdvisor or on Google Places; it's the customers. Smart businesses are building their online presence around these reviews.

This information abundance has changed the asymmetry of information between buyer and seller to parity or even a new asymmetry where the buyer has access to more information.

And this is the case in most industries. An example of an industry that changed radically is the travel industry. In the past, the traveller had very limited or no information at all when he wanted to book a flight or a hotel room and did rely 100% on travel agencies. Today the same traveller can check the prices online and look at the reviews and ratings from former customers. The information asymmetry that existed between the customer and the travel agency has disappeared completely. Some sites like Farecast, later bought by Microsoft, that started with the comparison of airline tickets, then later hotel rooms and concert tickets, TripAdvisor, Booking.com have even facilitated this shift.

The degree of asymmetry still differs from one industry to another and there are still some exceptions where the consumer is left a bit blind, but certainly not completely blind. Examples are the secondhand markets, where used goods are being exchanged and markets that are more complex such as legal services. These markets can still benefit from this information inequality, but they will also be challenged in the future. As Daniel Pink[11] points out in his book *To Sell is Human*, buyers aren't "fully informed" in the idealized way many economic models assume, but they are not the hapless victims of asymmetrical information as they once were.

The balance has indeed shifted, and in a world of information parity, the new guiding principle is "seller beware." The world is becoming so transparent, that you cannot hide any shortcomings. An unhappy customer has the potential to cause a lot of damage, especially if that person is influential. And that does not mean being a famous person, but a blogger or Facebook person with a big "crowd," maybe a thousand Facebook or LinkedIn friends and thousands of followers on Twitter.

We all know that much of the information online is not accurate by any means, but when finding your way in this abundance of information, it is sometimes very hard to appreciate what is right or wrong. The best

---

11   Daniel H.Pink is the author of five books about business, work, and
       management that have sold two million copies worldwide and have been
       translated into 34 languages

illustration is Wikipedia. In the past, people would get information from encyclopedias that had been written or checked by specialists in the field. Now, we rely on what has been written by the crowd of "non-experts." This has become the new truth!

People are connected everywhere. Mobile phones are continually on—not just for calls, but also to use the Internet. You are visiting an unknown place, turn on the app of TripAdvisor or Michelin and in a couple of seconds find the best Italian restaurant in the neighborhood, and see if some friends are there. You are waiting in line to pay at the grocery store and are checking in on Facebook on your iPhone to see what you friends have posted. In a couple of years we have made this unimaginable behavior ours. It's not only that what we might have done on our desktop we now do "on the road" using our smartphones, but we are also creating completely new behaviors, such as *showrooming*. Showrooming is a new phenomenon that Wikipedia defines as follows:

"Showrooming is the practice of examining merchandise in a traditional brick-and-mortar retail store without purchasing it, but then shopping online to find a lower price for the same item. Online stores often offer lower prices than their brick-and-mortar counterparts, because they

do not have the same overhead cost. Showrooming can be costly to retailers, not only in terms of the loss of the sale, but also due to damage caused to the store's floor samples of a product through constant examination from consumers." Showrooming is becoming a common practice.

Many apps make the showrooming process so easy that it only requires scanning the barcode of the product. The Columbia Business School did some research to find out if there was a correlation between showrooming and the price of the article. This study shows, the higher the price point, the more common showrooming gets.

For items above $500, more than half of the respondents did online research while in the shop but even more than one-quarter of the people did this for items under $50[12]! In terms of product types, the top category is electronics and appliances, followed by books and music, sporting goods, and hobbies. Even food and beverages are being researched!

What for the customer might look like "heaven" is becoming a nightmare for some retailers. Stores such as Nordstorm or Best Buy, in the US—which according to a survey by Harris Interactive, a leading

12   source: Colombia Business Shool, Showrooming and the Rise of the Mobile-Assisted Shopper, Matthew Quint and David Rogers, September 2013. http://www.gsb.columbia.edu/globalbrands/research/m-shopper-study

market-research firm, was the brick-and-mortar store most frequently showroomed—are trying to counteract these practices by changing their barcoding system or limiting Internet access inside their shops. But these tactics haven't been successful.

It is not only this new behavior of searching and comparing prices on a mobile devices that is on the rise, the mobile purchases, also known as m-commerce, has also seen a huge increase in the past year. According to comScore[13], purchases through mobile devices, have grown 23 percent year on year in the first quarter of 2014 compared to 12 percent on e-commerce. Amazon and Ebay confirm this trend.

This ubiquity of connection might be seen as a threat, but here again for smart retailers it opens huge opportunities. As we will discuss later in the chapter on the 10 Marketing Myths it is imperative to combine on- and off-line strategies. The physical store will more and more become a place where customers can experience the product and touch or feel it. Apple and Nespresso are great examples of what the future of retail might be.

Information Filters

We live in a world of "dis-traction." There is so much "going on," and it's becoming more difficult to stay focused and be present in both the private and business context. At home, you may be watching TV at the same time as looking at a so-called second screen, chatting on Facebook or even playing an online game. In a business meeting, people are conversing while continually checking e-mail on their smartphones. We are so easily distracted. There is an omnipresent digital clutter with the Internet, mobile phones, and tablets. All of these digital options are distracting people, who have difficulty focusing on one vehicle at a time. Dr. Edward Hallowell, a specialist in the field of attention deficit disorder calls today's affliction, "screensucking," or having to constantly be near some form of digital communication. He says it is like cigarette smoking: Once you get hooked, it is very difficult to break the habit.

---

13   comScore is an American Internet analytics company providing marketing data and analytics to many of the world's largest enterprises, agencies, and publishers

People are addicted to the digital clutter around them. If companies want to get through this clutter, they have to be very clever. When people are not even focusing on the important things, imagine if you want to attract them to things they do not even know they should care about.

Because of this immense clutter, we also have trained our brains to filter out the ads from the "more interesting" information. Just imagine the number of publicity inputs you might receive during a day, driving home, listening to the radio, reading the newspaper or some blogs, or watching television, and how few, if any, you remember! Shouting loud to get someone's attention is not working anymore. There are no "dead" moments anymore in our lives. Waiting in line means taking out our iPhone and launching some app to kill the time. This brings us to the next big impact.

Gamification

Digital games have mostly been geared toward younger male users. This trend is growing considerably. According to Frontier Group, teens drove 23 percent less miles in their cars over the last ten years[14]. Young males are now asking themselves, "Why drive? Why own a car? Why 'go' anywhere?" For the first time since the car was invented, young adults in the United States are not eager to drive. One reason is that driving is not so much fun anymore is there are so many rules on the roads. However the main reason is that instead of driving they would rather be communicating with others with their smartphone, reading Facebook, or gaming.

It's not only young people who like gaming, and it is not a new phenomenon. Women and men of all ages have always wanted to be entertained. With all the stress in the world, people want to play at home, at work, and school. Videogames make this easier than ever. As Gabe Zichermann points out in his book *The Gamification Revolution*[15], games might seem like part of the "problem of distraction"; they are in fact the one place where we increasingly find ourselves connected, and we enjoy this connection.

With so much going on to distract people, sellers need to find ways to attract buyers and keep their attention. Learning while playing was in fact our first school in life, and probably the most effective. Our educational system has not adopted it very well, but might reconsider this for the future. For companies, gaming might be the best way to engage the employees but also the customers.

As we will see later in this book, in the chapter on Marketing Myths and also in the online framework, educating and having people use our product or service is key to future success. To illustrate this, just look at www.thefuntheory.com, an experiment to stimulate people to take the stairs instead of the escalator. When stairs were made into musical keys, 66 percent more people chose the stairs over the escalator. Great gamified experiences that stimulate usage will definitely help build businesses. A game like Clash of Clans is a fantastic example how to

---

14   Frontier Group U.S. PIRG Education Fund, Transportation and the New Generation. Why Young People Are Driving Less and What It Means for Transportation Policy April 2012

15   Gabe Zicherman is the chair of GSummit where top gamification experts across industries gather to share knowledge and insight about customer & employee engagement and loyalty.

engage, or even get people addicted to it. Some of its principles should really be copied in your business strategy.

The Trust Factor

As Stephen M.R. Covey states in his book *The Speed of Trust*, *"The one thing which removed, will destroy the most powerful government, the most successful business, the most thriving economy, the most influential leadership, the greatest friendship . . . but on the other hand, if developed and leveraged has the potential to create unparalleled success and prosperity in every dimension of life. That one thing is TRUST."*

This is even more true in the anonymous digital world. When buyers go to small brick-and-mortar stores in their local towns, they know whom to trust. When they go to their doctors, they trust what these medical professionals have to say. Now, many consumers feel skeptical about buying online from someone they know nothing about. They have nearly unlimited options, so online sellers need to build and gain more trust from shoppers. Unless you have an established global brand most of the time as a seller you are anonymous online, so you have to create that trust and need an extra effort. Leadership expert John C. Maxwell[16] summed this up by saying, "People don't care how much you know until they know how much you care." That is, "I am only going to trust you if you show that you care about me." To establish this trust, businesses need to understand the customers' needs and define them better than they can do themselves. Sellers have to give value by educating customers and then motivate them to buy. And in this process of educating and creating trust, brands or individuals will position themselves as the "trusted expert."

This trust-building factor is of course not new, but only magnified due to the many choices, the transparency and anonymous aspect of the digital world. Compare this with dating, as it's a similar process: When people go on a date for the first time, they don't immediately plan on getting married. It's a process of getting to know and, especially, trust

---

16   John C.Maxwell is an American author, speaker, and pastor who has written more than 60 books primarily focusing on leadership

each other, and often reinforced by the opinion of others! This trust will be leveraged through social media. Never has social input been so important. Even for the purchase of a book we analyze the reviews of strangers.

These social "channels" play a crucial role in shaping our opinion on products, brands, and services. As of the first quarter 2014, Facebook had 1.28 billion monthly active users, and contrary to what one might think, they represent a nearly perfect mirror of the society, except perhaps for the more senior people, as we can appreciate in the graph below.

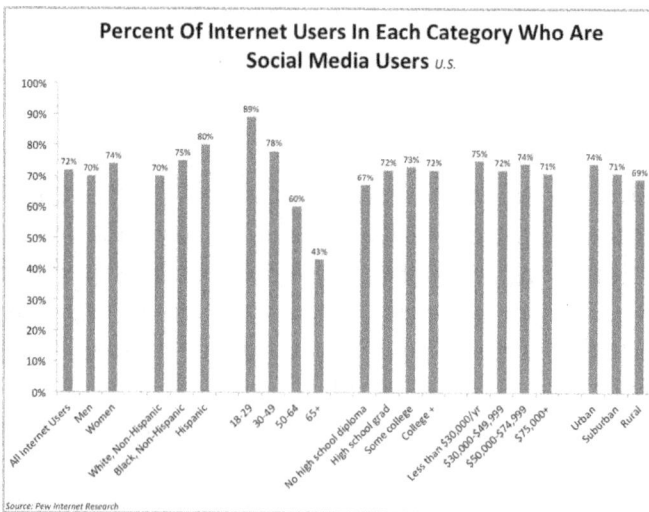

Illustration 1.4: Social Media Users

The Free Economy

In the FMCG—fast-moving consumer goods—world, free samples have always been used to introduce a new product in order to get first trials and have the potential buyer experience the product. Today the practice of giving free "samples" has taken on another dimension. What Chris Anderson predicted in his book Free: The Future of a Radical Price, is becoming a necessity to compete for some industries: give, give, and give more before you ask. In the app world, for example, this freemium model is by far the standard. More than 90 percent of apps are free. In most software-as-a-service (SaaS) businesses, too, the entry product is free, and you have to pay for the so-called pro or plus version, which usually unlocks more features or space. Most of the monetization is then based on only a percentage of the user base that effectively converts. Dropbox, for instance, is only making money on percent of its three hundred million users[17].

As more and more companies give their entry products away for free, everything online is expected to be free. If a company has no free entry product or service, it will have a hard time to motivate people. This business model is easier to adopt for SaaS or informational businesses that have marginal costs to produce or deliver the "free entry version" and therefore already rely on massive free adoption first. But other businesses too have to develop a freemium model, as this is the standard today.

It's also a way to lower barriers and risk for your prospects. You don't have to convince people. Your prospects try the product or service and decide to pay only if they find it valuable. It compensates for the initial lack of trust and should then be monetized through the conversion of free customers into paid ones and upsell afterwards. Having thousands or millions of users is nice but if you cannot monetize them your business may not be worth a lot.

The new customer on one hand has more information, is always connected, and on the other hand has sophisticated filters to only allow things of his interest to come through and seeks for trusted partners or brands when purchasing online. He is motivated by amusing games but wants everything for free. These are in my opinion the main characteristics of the new era customer, making it a lot harder to have loyal customers, if we even can speak about loyalty. The frequent-flyer methodology to keep customers hooked might have worked in the past, but today's companies cannot "control" this new "connected" customer anymore. But these are not the only changes in the business context.

On one hand some big brands like Kodak, Borders, and Blockbuster suffered from the changing business game and went bankrupt, because

---

17   https://www.dropbox.com/news

they could not adapt quickly to the new digital environment. On the other hand we all know the stories of YouTube, or more recently Instagram or Oculus, which was bought for $2 billion by Facebook[18]. In the past, to build a successful business, you needed mainly capital, resources, and labor. Today a fourth element has emerged: INFORMATION. This is certainly the most important element and has opened the way to a digital revolution with totally new players. In the past, and for some businesses even today, competitors were known. Now, however, this competition can appear from anywhere—from other countries, or from similar or completely different businesses. In the next pages I'll summarize what the fundamental changes are at the company side in order to better adjust your commercial plan.

---

18   http://mashable.com/2014/03/25/facebook-acquires-oculus-vr-for-2-billion/

New Companies

Globalization and Specialization

Instead of just competing against the other store down the street to attract the local prospects, the Internet has created a gigantic marketplace of three billion users that is likely to grow to six billion, and that is not burdened with the limitations of physical space. Even language and cultural barriers are disappearing. Import and export regulations might still protect some local markets artificially, mainly for food, textile, or drug related products, but even these hurdles cannot be sustained in the future. The new free economic marketplaces, like the European Community, will expand. In future years there might even be free marketplaces between the US, Canada, and Europe, making international trade even easier, creating a bigger marketplace to sell and purchase resources but also to offer and find labor; cheaper and or better than you can find locally. Platforms such as Elance, Odesk, or freelancer.com are facilitating this growth. Today millions of freelancers and businesses use these websites to find better suitable or cheaper candidates than they can find locally and this without the sometimes local constraints as local labor lows or high local tariffs.

The biggest impact of this global marketplace might be the emergence of super-niches. And this is for two reasons: One reason is that online there are no limitations of the physical shelf. No constraints to place the best-selling products on the top places to the detriment of other products. Online space is limitless and there are almost no inventory costs to place a product. This means that you can sell everything, even products that sell once a year. This concept is called the *long tail*. The same is also happening in newspapers. Physical newspapers had a limited number of pages, therefore only the top newsworthy stories got a spot. Today there is no limit anymore. In fact, today it's the contrary—

the more, the better. The other and more important reason is that a low-sales product can now be offered to the whole world and be a big success, and certainly if the one selling it is specializing in this niche. The big difference with the past is that a certain niche on a local level was not sustainable for most businesses, but with enough potential global buyers it is a different ball game. This is the "long tail" that can really be profitable. It's like the light energy of the sun versus that of a laser. Even if the energy from the sun is a thousand times stronger than the one from a laser, you can't make a hole with sunlight like you can with a laser! This is because of the focus of bundling all the light together. Online we see the same thing happening with niche players. Everything is specializing more and addressing more niche markets. Companies like Barkbox.com and Etsy.com are focusing in one niche, and thus it's easier for them to compete against the generalists. When people look at a keyword online they want the best information with the most depth.

Digital Disruption

Never has it been so easy to start a business. As I mentioned earlier, before the Internet you needed a minimum of capital and resources, and most of the time, expensive labor. Nowadays these ingredients are still there but have lost a lot of their importance, are readily available, or are a lot cheaper than a couple of years ago. This new business environment is possible because a lot of hurdles—or protection walls, which existed in the past, are becoming obsolete or have changed radically.

First, there are plenty of tools available that make launching a business seem like a kid's game. A couple of years ago, creating an animated video or creating a web- or e-commerce site would have meant a serious investment. Today you can record an HD quality video with an iPhone, or make professional looking animation with sites like Moovly.com, or set up your blog in an hour with WordPress, or create an e-commerce Magento, BigCommerce, or PrestaShop. Therefore the need to raise capital before launching an online site is becoming less relevant, but even if you do need money and don't find a business angel or investor, or the bank doesn't want to lend you the money, you can go to sites like Kickstarter or Indiegogo and raise the needed money there.

Second, you don't need a brick-and-mortar store. I don't mean you'll never need it, but investing in it is not a requirement anymore to start your business.

Third, and perhaps the most important but overlooked one, is the linking glue between your business and your customer: the infrastructure. The economical growth of most countries used to go hand in hand with the development of a good transportation infrastructure. For commercial exchanges we need roads, railways, airports. And this is still true today for off line businesses. In the online world today you don't need to build this infrastructure yourself from scratch. There are already excellent high traffic railways or roads such as Google, Apple, Facebook, YouTube, and Amazon. These sites are generating massive traffic and you just have to know how to take advantage of this and put your services and products before the traffic. To take an analogy with surfing: you leverage the speed of the waves.

This new environment allows even small players, like me, to start their own business and be a disruptor of established businesses that do not know how to play in this new environment. A good example is the publishing industry: Once very strong, the traditional print publishing industry is losing its edge. Even Amazon is selling more electronic than physical books. Welcome to the Kindle revolution. You do not need an intermediary to sell your books. Everyone can write a book and self-publish it. You sell it cheaper to the end customer and get more margins! And not only can you publish a book on Kindle, but also print and make an audio version. No need to have an intermediate anymore you can even print the books one by one.

And you don't have to make big innovations to be successful. In the 1940s, the Japanese learned how to clone American products. Today, the Chinese are doing the same. They are copying Western products, improving upon them, and selling them for less. There is no need to think about something completely new. A business can be just as successful by doing the same or better than competitors at a better rate. Online it has never been so easy. Usually we look at the big success stories like the iPad, Facebook, Twitter, Spotify as the ones that really were disrupters. However these are exceptions. There are many more successful copycats out there. One of the easiest strategies is to find a successful product or service, copy and improve some of the important benefits, and leverage better through your online marketing. The massive information that is available online allows anyone to "legally" steal the info or idea, copy the marketing strategy, and even allows targeting their customers. If you take a closer look at many games on the App Store you'll see the same framework over and over again. Take Supercell, the makers of Clash of Clans. They cloned this game into the very similar Boom Beach. Just make some new graphics and you have a new product. In sports they say never change a winning tactic and this is what works best.

Big Data

The amount and different sources of data is also changing the landscape. It's a fact that there is a lot more data, but the real breakthrough is that we are increasingly more able to analyze a variety of nonstandard data, in real time and find correlations. We can identify the big picture and get new insights. Analyzing data has been common practice in the decades since the introduction of the computer. What is new however is the ability to group various types of data, even non-standardized or messy data, and analyze that at a tremendous speed. Compare this with looking at a painting. In the past you could only look at a small piece of a painting one at a time. You could analyze these in detail, but you were missing the holistic view. Today we can take a couple of steps back and see the whole picture.

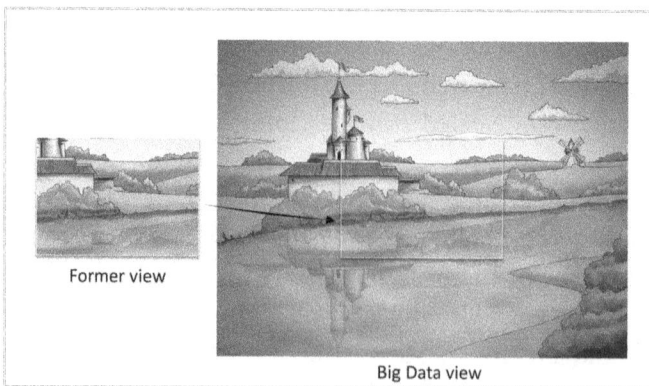

Former view

Big Data view

It's this aggregated view that enables a lot of new possibilities. In the past the analyses were mostly done to validate some hypothesis. The possibilities today are more to enable real-time actions. It's not to analyze why something is like that, but what to do if something happens.

To illustrate this: In 2009 when the swine flu or H1N1 virus broke out, the whole world feared a terrible pandemic like the Spanish flu of 1918 that killed more than fifty million people.

The objective was to slow its spreading and all medical centers in the world asked their doctors to report all cases. The problem was that the picture of the spread of the disease was always a week or two outdated. On the other hand, Google had analyzed some correlations between previous seasonal flus between 2003 and 2008 and what people searched online out of the three billion searches every day. Out of the fifty million most common search terms they identified the forty-five words that correlated with the flu. And with these same search terms Google was able to predict one week before the cases were identified where the swine flu was spreading. By the way, most of that data was available to everyone! The possibilities that will emerge out of big data are endless and will allow industries to transform their business models. Telefonica, the Spanish telecommunications giant, for instance is selling aggregated data they capture from their customers to real estate companies in order to identify the best retail locations.

We see that the world has changed due to the technological changes: The customer's ability to get his desires fulfilled and his buying process have changed. He is less loyal due to an increased transparency. On top of that there are fewer barriers for new competitors to enter our space. But we have also access to more data, don't need much capital and for the clever businesses there are also more and new opportunities. But therefore you have to also change your Marketing and Sales strategies. This is what the next chapter is about. Get rid of the old Marketing paradigms, I call them the Marketing Myths. Some of these are more obvious, other might surprise you if you are used to "old school" marketing. So, be open to listen to new music and get ready for online Marketing 3.0

PART 2

The Pillars of Online Marketing 3.0

*"If you only read the books that everyone else is reading,
you can only think what everyone else is thinking"*

Haruki Murakami, Norwegian Wood

The world and technology are changing at a tremendous speed and it is very difficult to keep up to speed if you are not living it in the trenches. We have seen in the previous chapter how this affected the buying process. Theses radical changes have a tremendous impact on how we should market and sell our products and services. Since the arrival of the Internet, social media, and big data old school marketing does not work anymore. Indeed some mindsets of traditional marketing are no longer applicable today even if many academic institutions still teach the old approach. Of course some of the foundations of Marketing like the four *P*s: product, price, promotion, and place, are not dead, but it is how you set up your strategy and tactics that are new. Today you still hear a number of misconceptions or "myths" about marketing. This chapter will demystify the most important misconceptions and explain how you should plan your sales and marketing today. It also sets the stage for the underlying framework later on in the book, which gives a step-by-step sales and marketing system especially suited to the fast-changing marketplace.

CHAPTER 2

The Marketing Myths

"If you don't drive your business, you will be driven out of business"

Bertie Charles Forbes

Myth #1: Branding Is the Building Block of All Marketing

It is completely wrong to have branding as your primary marketing goal. Branding should be a byproduct. Austen Riggs, a famous psychiatrist said, "Happiness is only a byproduct of successful living." Well, so is branding. You cannot "buy" happiness, and you cannot "buy" a brand. It's impossible to have a good brand without all the other elements in place. Branding is the personality of your service or product. It is created through the interaction with your customers and prospects. It's the result of a relationship. Whether you are a person or a company. It cannot be created using billboard advertising bragging that your business is the best. You have to deserve it. Your relationship should focus on providing substance and qualitative value, not on image building.

So why do people love branding so much?

The corporate world people LOVE branding for two reasons. The first is because it's what everyone does and thinks they should do. Advertising agencies are continuously stalking to try to fill some space in newspapers or television. So as a marketer it is the obvious way. If you don't spend money on branding and the product doesn't work you might get blamed that no one knows about your product. This leads us to the second reason: The most positive effect of "traditional" branding is the effect *inside* the company. All employees love branding, because it makes them feel more important. Employees might call their relatives or friends to ask if they saw their brand campaign.

Many companies have gone bankrupt because they felt they needed to build a brand in order to sell. But on the other hand, even in the off-line world we see great brands that achieved the branding through the creation of excellent customer experiences. Take Starbucks, for example. They created what they call the "third home," and spent a lot of time and money, not on the pure branding, but on the relationship. Through this relationship building, a brand was born.

You cannot create a brand before you create a business: Your business creates your brand.

Why People love Branding

In the late 1800s, the US department store magnate John Wanamaker said, "Half of the money I use on advertising is wasted; the trouble is, I do not know which half." Marketers living in the nineteenth century and even the earlier twentieth century had a difficult time determining the best way to spend their marketing money, since there were few tools to help. Marketing was like putting money in a slot machine. You had a certain probability to win, but did not know what really worked best. There was no direct correlation between the ad and results. Today this should not be the case. Every penny you invest can and should be tracked. Spending on advertising should be seen as putting money in a vending machine. You *choose* what you want, you *know* what it *costs*, and you get the *results* you expected. Say you put $1 in a vending machine and choose a Coke, what is the result? A Coke. Same in advertising: You put in $1 and get a specific target customer, that you know will result in, let's say, $50 in sales over time. If you know how to monetize this customer over a lifetime, you know what your leverage factor is. You put in $1 and multiply this by two for example. If you spend $2,000, you get $4,000. Then you optimize your strategy and get three times the amount in return. So, you spend your $4,000 and get $12,000. This means that your budget shouldn't be limited!

Slotmachines versus Vending Machines

Most ad agencies do not like online advertising. And this is for various reasons:

First, the amount spent is normally only a fraction of the off-line budget spent on off-line advertising and part of their business model is based on a fee from this budget. Second, now there is full transparency and you can directly correlate an agency's work with the results you get from your direct-response marketing. Creating a friendly or humorous ad that is only partially responsible for the company's improved results is not enough. Ad agencies are now liable for these returns. Also, with such tracking tools, less start-up money is involved. You should really start testing and only improve and leverage when you get the expected results. This is how successful businesses proceed. No $100,000 budgets to start with—only when the results prove it is a good investment! Third, many agencies are still are not up to speed with the new marketing and sales strategies and still defending their old model.

Remember, we live in a world of full transparency, where you do not control what customers hear about you. People post tweets about their bad and good experiences. You cannot hide anymore or try to brainwash them with lots of messages. So, focus on the relationship and your customers will "rave" about your brand, and it will build itself.

Myth #2: Your Website Is the Most Important Part of Your Online Marketing

When I worked for Shell in Network Planning and identifying where to invest in a new service station, I learned the three key indicators that would guarantee the success of the station. These were:

1. Location

2. Location

3. Location

The World Wide Web is not different—people need to find you easily. Traffic is one of the essential building blocks of your online

Is this your Website?

strategy. You do not want your website to be lost in the middle of the online desert. And except for the big top brands, too often we forget that people do not know us and so will not find us. Either you go "*where the traffic is*" or "*you build the traffic.*" Take the analogy to the off-line world: If you want to be where the traffic is, you put your retail store on Times Square in New York, Oxford Street in London, or on the Champs Elysées in Paris, and you pay big money for that. Or, you decide to put your store in a cheaper location like an outlet. You pay less, but need to "build" the roads and create the traffic that might take a lot longer.

In the online world, you have to do both: Be on the traffic highways and create traffic. The good news is that you can take advantage of the existing megahighways like Google, Apple's iTunes Store, Facebook, YouTube, or Amazon, divert this traffic to you and get quick results without breaking the bank as in the off-line world. You also have to focus on building your traffic. Traffic generation is really one of the most crucial parts of your strategy. Most businesses forget this. They spend too much time and energy trying to make their website perfect, even though nobody might ever find it or might immediately leave upon arrival. Most companies consider their websites as the shopwindow. In the off-line world, a shop window is to get people INSIDE your shop. This is the main purpose. However, online your shop windows are the many other pieces, like ads that will bring your people to a web page. Once they are on your site, the users are already INSIDE, so your objective is different! The main objective of your website is to *convert* the incoming traffic either by getting the e-mails of the visitors or by selling something. So, do not clutter your site with lots of distractive elements. Do not spend all your time and money in creating a megawebsite.

On average, people spend eight seconds on your website.

This is an average! Below you can see research results on the probability of leaving a website after a certain time. We see that it is crucial to get people over the twenty-second mark. However, only 2 percent of the visitors will do so. Recent research indicates that people will form an initial impression of your landing page within fifty milliseconds. Not a lot of time to make a first impression!

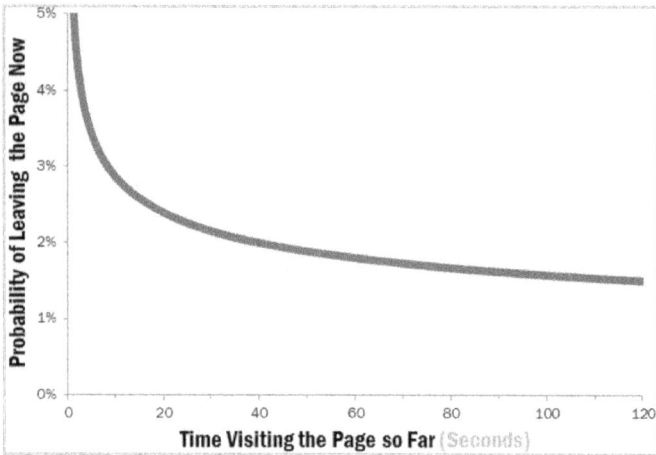

Illustration 2.1: Probability of staying on a certain webpage

Every page only has ONE objective. And often this will be to capture the e-mail of the visitor. Visitors rush through web pages and have the time to read only a quarter of the text on the ones they actually visit. Therefore, you need to make sure that your message is "to the point" and "teasing." Do not clutter your pages with too much information. The more clutter you place on the page the more difficult it gets. People take only a few seconds to make a decision on whether or not to stay on the site. People read at an average speed of three hundred words per minute. If someone takes eight seconds to decide whether to stay or leave, you have approximately forty words to convince your visitors! Or, use attractive photos or videos. Videos are definitely the best content you can have. People love to watch videos, hence the success of YouTube. Make your videos engaging with a call to action. Your goal is to convert all visitors to your site. Your objective is to get their e-mail, which often means giving them something in return.

Myth #3: Try to Reach as Many People as You Can to Get a Massive List

We usually want to sell to as many people as we possibly can and do this as fast as we can. You do not want to exclude any potential customer because you fear that you will lose opportunities to sell. However this broad-based approach is one of the major problems and one of the biggest paradoxes in marketing. One size does not fit all, especially online.

Today we have the false perception that sending out e-mail is free. Why should we leave some prospects or customers out? Perhaps they may buy something. So we end up sending big blasts of mail or targeting more people than we can possibly reach. The problem is that to appeal to that audience we have to find the commonalities of this audience. The more people in there, the more general our message or offer becomes. So what we end up doing is broadcasting. We have a general message that appeals vaguely to the big group. This results in less interested people or even annoyed people.

This broadcasting even has negative side effects. People are continuously bombarded with e-mails, advertising, so if someone shouts so loud that they look but it has very little interesting information chances are that the door for this "advertiser" will be closed forever.

Also, if you e-mail or advertise to a big list emphasizing many different features or benefits, your target might be interested in some of them; but may have the impression that he will pay too much for the service or product because he does not need all these!

Narrow Your Target

What we have to do is narrow the target group and focus on that smaller segment. In an ideal world this is ONE person. In a one-on-

one conversation you can indeed talk directly to the real needs and aspirations of your prospect. And here you can really trigger the interest of the prospect if you know him well, know his desired outcome, the topics that motivate him, the languages he speaks, the channels he listens to. Knowing your prospects makes it easier to control the scene. If you want to be the number 1 in the world for a certain topic, you should start by being the local number 1. Isn't that the way a Rafael Nadal or a Tiger Woods became number one? By first winning the local championships?

When President Obama first ran for office, for example, his marketing focused on several different Facebook target markets by ethnic group. A distinct message was delivered to each of these groups of potential voters. With today's technology, this is very easy to do. You do not need to use—and should not use—one large channel to broadcast your message. Rather, you should focus down, find each of the niches, and communicate with each one of them in a different way. The message will appeal to their particular interests. This helps eliminate the clutter that surrounds the potential customers. You are sending a specific message to them that will break through all the distractions.

Myth #4: The Main Objective of Marketing Is to Communicate and Promote My Products or Services

Marketing is usually associated with humorous advertisements and communication to promote a product or service and typically is used in the "launch phase." The process is usually like this:

You have a great idea.

You find out how to materialize it.

You create it and

You market the product . . .

. . . to find out that it doesn't work!

This is the process that most companies use, but it is also the main reason why most start-ups go bankrupt. Even big corporations fail in their product launches.

Let's say you open a restaurant that makes the best and most tasty meals. If the people sitting down at the table are not hungry or do not like the type of food being offered, what you make is a moot point. The leading restaurants are not necessarily those that are the most fancy or exotic. If the customer is not craving food—is not hungry—it does not matter what delicacies are being served.

Many companies think that having a good, well-thought-out, well-crafted product is all that is needed to succeed. They assume that the consumer will like and desire their product or service just because it is a good idea or that it is made with excellent craftsmanship. These businesses, however, soon find out that there is no market for their product. Marketing is not recognized as the most important part of the business and as an integral part of setting the strategy. Marketing is often seen as being secondary to having a good product. When you hear, "Now that we have a product, how are we going to market it?" it's too late! You cannot bring marketing into the game after you have designed the product. You have to think marketing from the start.

Of course many companies will do some classic market research before launching the product, asking people about their "intention" to buy. The harsh reality is that intention to buy is one of the worst predictors of success. Many people would like to lose weight or leave their job and start a company on their own, but how many really do it? Intention and action are very different. Taking action requires effort and is painful, and opening your wallet and putting money on the table is painful. You cannot rely on intention only. However in the past this was the only reliable way to test out things. Today there are other

| Your product or service | | | | |
| educational toys | | | Get ideas | M |

| Ad group ideas | Keyword ideas | | | ⬇ D |

Search terms		Avg. monthly searches ?	Competition ?	Suggested bid ?	Ad
educational toys	〱	8,100	High	€0.70	

1 - 1 of 1 K

Keyword (by relevance)		▼ Avg. monthly searches ?	Competition ?	Suggested bid ?	Ad
jigsaw puzzles	〱	165,000	Medium	€0.40	
kids games	〱	165,000	Medium	€0.46	
toys	〱	90,500	Medium	€0.35	
games for kids	〱	90,500	Medium	€0.64	
education	〱	74,000	Low	€2.99	
melissa and doug	〱	60,500	Medium	€0.59	
toy	〱	40,500	Low	€0.30	
crafts for kids	〱	33,100	Medium	€1.00	
educational games	〱	33,100	Medium	€1.28	

Illustration 2.2: Google searches for educational toys and related words

ways, and you have to find out before your product is perfectly crafted. Market research can now be done in a more scientific way. Google will tell you how many people are actively searching for some products or services. You can see if companies are paying for keywords in AdWords, meaning that they are generating some business out of them. You can see if some apps are making money—look at the top grossing apps— even if they are free. This research is based on facts not on intentions.

In chapter three on ABC foundation, we will go into depth about how to do this online market research, but right now, you'll just get a taste of it.

Imagine we want to find out how many times per month "educational toys" is looked up.

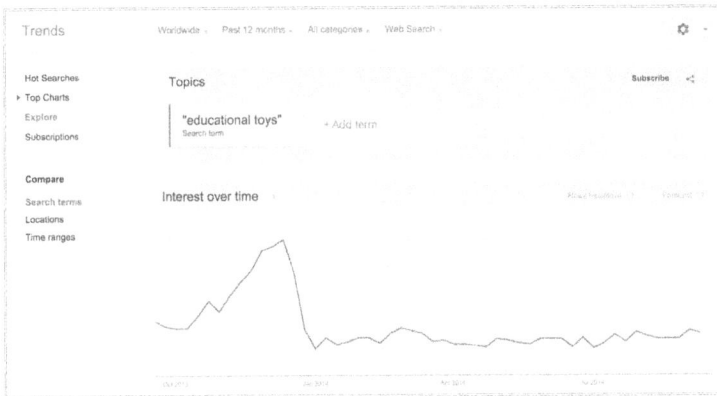

Illustration 2.3: Monthly Google searches for "educational toys"

There are many great tools you can pay for to do this, but for now the Google Keyword Planner tool in AdWords will be enough. http://adwords.google.com/KeywordPlanner

As you can see in the example here for "educational toys," we have on average 8,100 people in the United States searching actively for this keyword. No surprise, there's a huge seasonality peak before and during the Christmas period. These keywords are very powerful and really tell you what people are actively looking for. But, even more interesting, is to look at the related words *jigsaw puzzles* (with 165,000 searches). You can do this analysis for any geographical area and in any language.

The suggested bid to purchase a specific keyword will then give you an indication what companies are bidding to get click through and the traffic from these active searches. If companies pay for a keyword, it means that they are "monetizing" this traffic. This can be your first indication that there is potential. Of course you will have to look at the level of competition and the ease of entering this market.

But online research does not stop with keyword analysis. You can find a lot about your potential customers, who they are, where they hang out, and how easily you can reach them.

This will help you with the "packaging" and "communication" of your product.

After you have crafted a product that you know has a potential market and should sell, you make a first version as quickly as possible and ship it to the market. Then you can start testing as quickly as possible. You start selling on your website and find out if customers are really willing to pay. In some cases you can do this even before you really have a product. Think of designing a course or selling products that you don't even have in stock! If customers don't buy, then you know you have to change, adapt your product, or stop. But if they do buy, you optimize, optimize, and optimize again. And only after various iterations, when you know that if you put $1 in your advertising you get a multiple out of it you can scale. You will then find out if it converts and start to improve it to find the sweet spot. Ryan Holliday[19], in his book *Growth Hacker Marketing* calls it finding the PMF: the Product Market Fit. Starters, as he said, have no big marketing budgets to launch their product, so they have to rely on the leverage effect of *virality*[20]. This means that people will share and talk about your product so that you really do not need a marketing budget. Virality is not something easy to obtain, and it cannot be an objective to make a viral video. There are indeed some fundamentals

---

19   Ryan Holiday is an American author, writer, and marketer. He is the media strategist behind authors Tucker Max and Robert Greene, and the Director of Marketing for American Apparel

20   virality is defined as The tendency of an image, video, or piece of information to be circulated rapidly and widely from one Internet user to another. Oxford dictionary

of what makes something viral, but if your product is not a right fit for the market it won't. So you have to find out what the markets want, make a first "prototype," and launch it to the market before it is perfect. Don't waste all the money in perfecting the product and launch it one year later to find out if it works or not. I've seen so many failures that could have been successes had the product been launched earlier and been adapted to the market reality and desires. Paradoxically most big companies have big budgets to launch products and many of them think they can create a market for their product. But few have the vision as Steve Jobs had. You have to understand thoroughly what people really want and test this as quickly as possible in the marketplace to see if it works or not. The key is to learn quickly if you are going to fail or succeed. Failing fast is one of the best strategies. Small companies with small budgets have no other choice and often do a better job at this.

Some cultures, like mine in Belgium, have an adversity to failure. It should be perfect from the start. But failure is important and is inherent with testing. If you want effective online marketing you need to test and then test again to see what approach works best.

Test, measure, take the best, make improvements, retest, optimize, and then scale.

Testing is Key

Testing is hugely important. Not so long ago, hardly anyone could do this. Today you can test your headlines, your sales copy, your offer, and even your "unfinished" product. There is no reason not to try to improve some parts of the marketing process. Testing is an iterative process. Imagine you have 3 advertising pieces to test. Let's call them A, B and C. After some exposure and getting enough data you find out that B is the one that outperforms the other two. Now you take B and change small things on it and make versions B1, B2 and B3. Now you find out B3 is the best and create versions B31, B32, B33. Learn to test everything even if it works and try to optimize it.

There are many performance indicators that you will analyze and try to improve through testing. Some of the most important ones are:

- Click-through rate (CTR): The percent of people that click on your ads.

- Opt-in (conversion) rate: The percent of visitors to your website that leave their e-mail in exchange for some *value piece*, like a report, access to a video, a document, …

- Sales (conversion) rate: The percentage of visitors buying

- E-mail delivery rate: The percentage of e-mails that get into the inbox.

- E-mail open rate: The percentage of sent e-mails that get opened

- E-mail click-through rate: The percentage of people that received the e-mail and clicked on it.

I'll go through most of them in detail in the chapters about the sales & marketing funnel.

To illustrate a bit more the concept let's take click-through rate (CTR), as an example. You can do your ad testing on different headlines, different images, and small changes in copy. It is important to only test one item at a time. Do not compare, for instance, one ad with a different photo, different copy, and headline at the same time.

You should not only focus on the improvement of one performance indicator, but have a look at the overall results. A small change in one parameter can have a big impact on the total results.

You might improve your click through rate by optimizing ads making them more appealing, but not totally related to your target group and find out that you get indeed more clicks but that these clicks are not converting in to sales or people opting in. Your marketing should work like a vending machine. In a vending machine you put $1 in the machine and choose a Coke. In a well-oiled marketing machine you know that putting in $1 will get you a multiple. And your objective is to improve this multiple as much as you can.

In addition, you always need to test out different types of media. None will be perfect from the beginning. Which traffic source brings the most visitors, and who are the most qualified visitors? You do not have to launch your website as soon as it goes up. You can spend some time getting feedback from small tests and optimizing the results. You can also do a beta test. This is a term or practice that is common in the software world. You launch your product, often for free, to a small group of users. Even if the product is not hundred percent ready, to see how it work, get feedback from the users and find out how you can improve it before you do the real launch. With the current tools, you can conduct tests and get results so quickly that it is easy to try different approaches. You do not have to wait for months or even a year to go by to see if something needs to be done differently.

1. Analyze if there is a market

2. Identify the various niches

3. Analyze if the niches are willing to pay and how much

4. Identify the real needs and what the competitor's products are

5. Make a better product than what currently exists in the market

6. Test it out

7. Improve or stop

8. Repeat 6 and 7 till you have a "product that sells itself"

9. Start the communication and promotion

10. Optimize the communication and sales flow

11. Scale

"Marketing is to a business what oxygen is to a body." It must be considered key to a company's success.

Myth #5: To Attract Customers You Have to Spend a Lot and Shout Louder Than the Competition

Previously, to get someone's attention, a gentle tap on the shoulder was enough. Today you need to hit at full force with a sledgehammer or . . . understand your target niche and attract them with value.

But that requires you to understand your target audience very well. You have to narrow your niche, know what these people want, where you can find them, and be laser-focused when contacting them rather than using broad and expensive media. By narrowing down your niche, you can better understand these people and know where they hang out, what they read, and what they actively search for! It's not about shouting loud through big media campaigns or by sending out hard-sell advertisements. Instead, it is being clever and teasing your niche with great value in the places where you can find them.

You don't have to spend thousands of dollars and kill an ant with an atomic bomb!

You have to know how to leverage the online superhighways. Take Google, for instance. What are all the keywords that people search for in Google? You have to analyze people's searching patterns and what they specifically are looking for and offer value and a solution—for free—to those searchers. Another way might be by creating a Kindle book on Amazon, or via an app on iTunes, or being in front of them in the Facebook News Feed.

These are the highways where you can cherry-pick the people in your niche. It will cost you some money, but nothing compared to the mass media budgets and will quickly bring positive returns. The key is then to track and improve your campaigns and follow up with your lead.

Using these highways is as if you have an off-line shop, deciding whether to put your store in a commercial mall that is well advertised and gets thousands of customers every day or in a small town where you will have to slowly grow the business until people come to you. You have to really understand the way to target people on those highways. Google is like the Yellow Pages of the past. When consumers were looking for something particular, they would use this big yellow book and search for a solution. Being listed was crucial for any business. Today a listing in the phone book has been replaced by Google searches. These searches might only represent 5 or 10 percent of the total potential customers. But the ones that are searching on Google are the best prospects because they are already proactively looking for a solution that you are offering.

Facebook, on the other hand, is more like the off-line coffee shop where people are sitting around and talking to one another. If your product can be found in the conversations going on in the coffee shop, you might consider it an ideal place to interrupt anyone interested in your topic. People read Facebook as a personalized newspaper today. And for you as an advertiser, this is one of the best places to where you can buy laser-focused cheap traffic, certainly if your product is related to hobbies, music, media, or fashion or entertainment.

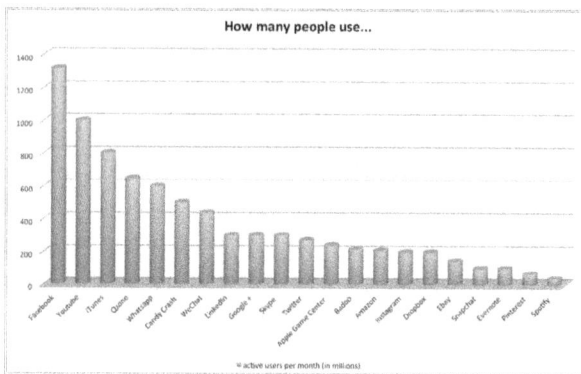

Illustration 2.4: Million users of some high traffic sites

Besides Google and Facebook there are many of these highways today. In graph 2.4 you see the estimated users of various sites that generate loads of traffic, with millions of users that you might benefit from.

Successful online marketing is not about spending the most money, it's about spending it cleverly!

Myth #6: The More You Push, the More You Sell

Too many organizations see marketing as a numbers game. They say, "I will hire a large number of salespeople and do cold-calling or even cold-visiting. The more arrows I shoot, the more times I will hit my target." Not only is this reasoning wrong, it can have very negative effects. First, it is cost-inefficient because of the large staff to pay and second, and maybe even more important is the danger that you will repel most potential customers. Most customers might not be ready to buy from you when you are selling and by pushing you are not going to get positive results. They will have negative feelings about your product or service. You have to understand that *"People love to buy, but hate to be sold to."*

The funny thing is no one likes to be sold to. Who doesn't hang up when getting a telemarketing sales call? But still we think our business is different and our customers will buy if we push them hard enough. The same logic is being done online: E-mail is free, so why not massively e-mail them?

"Hard-selling" is not effective anymore

You need to nurture your prospects and provide valuable free information in order to establish trust before making your pitch. Give them great content and then lead them toward their desired end result. People want to be led, even though they do not admit it. They just do not want to be pushed. If you have a good relationship, they will take your hand and you can lead them anywhere. But you have to be patient. Compare this to a chess game. Start with the end in mind, winning the king. A great chess player will go backward and identify all the moves that lead to a winning end! It's a step-by-step process. You have to be patient and go at the pace of your customer, not yours.

Many times I hear that online marketing is easier than off-line marketing. But this is not the case. Online marketing is anonymous and difficult and much more competitive. In the past, due to geographical constraints you had to go to brick-and-mortar stores, even some that you did not like. There was no alternative. These physical constraints were protecting many businesses.

Today, with a click you can change your provider to one of the many options on the web.

Also, and perhaps more importantly, in the "past," when you signed a contract with a customer, you immediately received a "pot" filled with money. Today signing a contract means getting an e-mail or an "empty pot." The gold will not be there. You can fill the pot only if you slowly, but surely, build a platform with your buyers. Step-by-step you acquire this customer's trust and then, and only then, sell and upsell.

People can be convinced in two ways, explicitly and implicitly. Explicitly is when you have to argue and prove that your service or product is good. Like cold-selling: "You should buy this product because of this and this." Implicitly is when the customer is convinced without you really convincing or giving proof. People who are convinced implicitly do not easily change their mind. They are convinced you are the best and will remain very loyal. If you convince people explicitly they may end up doing one transaction with you but leave you afterwards. Your goal should be to invest in them to get lifetime customers. Therefore it is so crucial to build that trust and try to lower the risks for your prospect to do business with you. Create goodwill and when they start to trust you, let them make a first small transaction. Then, when the relationship is more established, they will make larger transactions. Companies have to adapt to the new mindset of free and have a freemium strategy. As a marketer, you need to lower the risk to do business with the customer. A first step in this direction is a full money-back guarantee and free shipping, but this has even become the norm today. If you are convinced about the quality of your product the ideal way should be to give it away and only start charging when your customer gets the desired results!

Myth #7: I Have to Be Blogging, Tweeting, and Posting on Facebook Every Day!

You hear about companies that hire conversation managers or professional tweeters. They invest a lot of time and energy, but soon get frustrated when they don't see any results on their investment. Others prefer to completely forget about social media, because they do not understand it or are afraid that something negative will be said on their pages.

Both practices are not good. Social media cannot be ignored. It is here and will stay for many more years, whether you like it or not. It is the *way* you use social media that is key! You cannot be posting or tweeting for the sake of it or hope that you will get better brand recognition. You see too many pages bragging about their brands or asking you on Facebook to *like* their page. Why should I like a page on kite surfing if I am not interested in it? Using social media has to be done in the light of the overall marketing strategy. Basically there are four strategic objectives that you should use social media for:

- Lead generation
- Leverage
- Search engine optimization (SEO)
- Education

Lead Generation

Many social media platforms can be seen as the new personalized newspapers. If you know who your audience is, you can get in front of it very easily. Today, Facebook allows us to place advertising inside the News Feed right in the middle of your prospects' friends' feed. If you target the right audience, this is very powerful. Like people in a coffee shop, they are susceptible to distraction. You can distract them easily if you are targeting the right audience with the right message and motivation! The objective here is not to stay on Facebook but to take people out of the social media and to your website! How to effectively advertise on Facebook will be covered in great detail in the chapter on traffic building.

Leverage

Once you have followers, you can create an environment that leverages your content or even advertises to their connections. If you offer value content, especially videos, photos, or well-written and interesting articles, your followers will want to share this content. They will like your content and comment on it. This is key. Everyone has hundreds or even thousands of friends. If they share your information, other people will see it, and recognize that it is coming from a trusted friend. In their eyes you are not promoting yourself, but their friend is sharing something of interest. Besides that, advertising on Facebook also gets you meta-effects with lots of "likes" as a bonus, which create a huge Facebook base. This is only effective when you already have a large number of fans. So if you don't, you will have to work on it. Don't let that be your main strategy. Keep it as a second priority. Ask your existing customers to like you in exchange for something. Another way is to import your actual customers inside the social platforms. Facebook allows you to import your existing customer base and create a Facebook audience with matched e-mails or telephone numbers.

SEO

Search engine results are based on algorithms that are constantly changing. Services like Google are putting more and more weight on the number of "social activities," such as "likes," comments, reviews, and shares. The more and better the comments, the higher you will be ranked. Even iTunes and Amazon are not only relying on downloads or sales to rank apps or books, but they take the reviews heavily into account. These are the new type of testimonials. Companies that are just starting a Facebook page want to quickly get a lot of likes. But don't take the wrong approach. Do not send out e-mails saying, "Please like my page." Target the right audience and give them something in return for their "like."

Education

Nurturing your prospects and customers with good content is crucial. This has to be done through various channels. The main one will definitely be e-mail for most companies, but social media will be an excellent complement to the 'old' e-mail.

The bottom line is that you have to use social media, but you have to be strategic and use it the right way.

Myth #8: You Should Split the Offline and Online Strategies

Somehow, along the way, the off-line and online marketing campaigns of many companies became separate. Sometimes businesses are afraid they will be cannibalizing their marketing by combining off- and online efforts—especially businesses with networks, like retail stores. Sometimes a company might be reluctant to combine on- and offline, because the stores might perceive online as a competitive channel. This is a huge mistake. It is essential to find the right strategy that connects all the dots. If you are lucky to have a brick-and-mortar shop or chain, take advantage of this. It has never been as important to combine both of these marketing efforts into a unified strategy. The line between online and offline is not clear anymore. Showrooming and searching online before going to the physical shop are part of our buying behavior, and this should be reflected in our marketing. In communicating with the customer, remember buyers may have different preferences and do not respond in the same way. They need to be reached with a variety of marketing efforts.

Work in both ways: Get the customers' e-mails from the shops and nurture them online, but also send them back to the shops. Apps, for instance, can be an excellent vehicle to bring new potential customers to the brick-and-mortar stores. A restaurant can ask their customers to rate their experience on an iPad together with the bill. If the restaurant gets the customer's e-mail address, it can send them information on promotions or special events. Similarly, you can ask for your customer's physical "snail mail" address and surprise them with something like a book as a free gift. Also, do not forget about traditional marketing tools. For instance, direct marketing is once again gaining in popularity and working better than in the past. Even Amazon is now using magazine advertisements in print magazines to promote themselves. People are so used to e-mail that receiving something in the postal mail can be more effective. Send a postcard via snail mail that encourages potential customers to go online and get more information or to enter a contest.

Another reason to combine on- and off-line is that despite the huge worldwide connectivity, there are still potential customers who are not so connected to the Internet and not on Facebook: the market of seniors over sixty years. How will you reach them? If you use off-line marketing to help seniors go online, you will build strong relationships with them. Give them a tablet or mobile phone app for free, show them how to work with it, and they will be very loyal to you.

The goal is to combine the online and off-line worlds.

Myth #9: Mobile is Marketing on a Small Screen

Even if we agree that a smartphone is like our third arm and that mobile cannot be left out of our daily habits, still very few companies have a mobile strategy or dedicate resources to create an app. As you see in illustration 2.5, not even half of the big corporate companies have any mobile optimization.

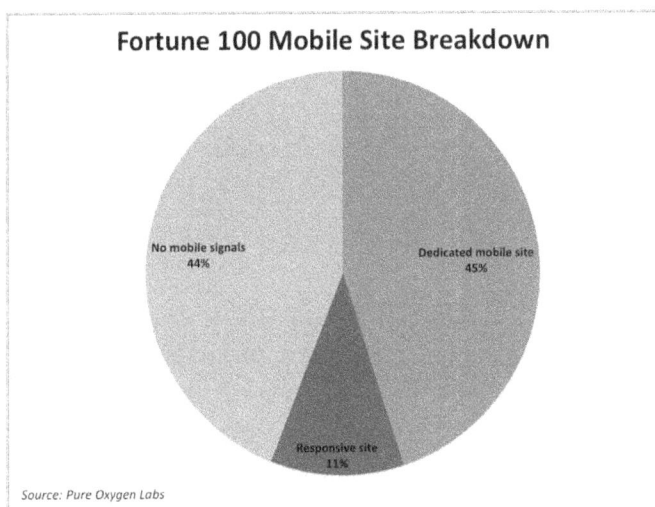

Fortune 100 Mobile Site Breakdown

No mobile signals 44%

Dedicated mobile site 45%

Responsive site 11%

Source: Pure Oxygen Labs

Illustration 2.5: Percentage of Companies with Dedicated Mobile Site

And if they do, they consider mobile as marketing on a small screen. You can indeed just create a special smaller version of your website and rely on that. But then you are losing the big benefits and opportunities that you can get by creating a dedicated app. You will have more and better interactions as you and your buyers can interface through different digital vehicles. An app is not another website. It is an important tool for your overall marketing strategy.

People love apps; they download more apps than they visit websites. I don't think I could have reached 1.3 million kids through a website as easily as I've done with my app business, and this without a business that supports the app business.

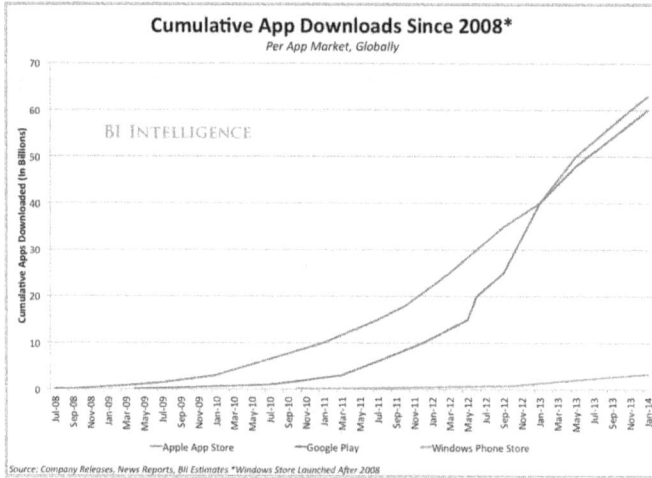

Illustration 2.4: Cummulative App Dowloads

In September 2013, Apple CEO Tim Cook revealed some updated milestones for his company's app store: Cumulative app downloads had surpassed 60 billion. The latest estimates say that there are more than 1 million apps available in Apple's App Store and a similar amount on Google Play. Even though that figure might seem huge and daunting if you want to put your app there, compare this with the number of website pages. A study made at the University of Tilburg in the Netherlands estimated that in November 2013 there were 2.18 billion web pages. Compare these figures: 2 million apps versus 2.18 billion webpages !

Having your app out there has many advantages: Most website visitors will never come back, but apps are different. When you decide to download it they are on your smartphone. You might remove it but if I know how to engage you and hook you in, you are a longtime customer. And it is an incredible communication and relationship vehicle. It's a huge opportunity! If people allow you to send them push notifications, you can build that into your app, and the communication can automatically be sent from inside the app, based on some predefined triggers. Even if the amount of people allowing push notifications might seem low as you can see in illustration 2.6., due to the "spamming" by some developers, you can impact personal behavior, analyze it, and produce better results in terms of product development and communication. Content-focused apps have generally a high opt-in rate of up to 70 percent, while marketing or gaming apps, which have less reason to send push ads, see lower acceptance rates in the 30-percent range. In the same way you combine on- and off-line strategy, try to combine apps with websites and other channels.

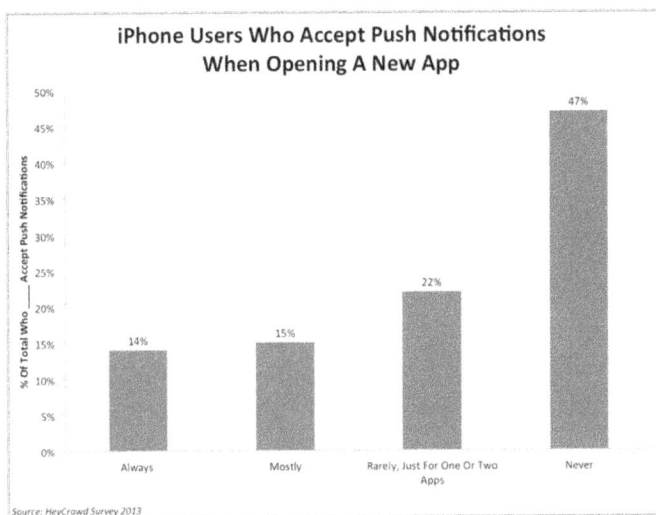

Illustration 2.6: Push Notification Acceptance

People often ask me what kind of app they should make. I sometimes hear or see the craziest ideas. My advice is to keep it simple. Think of how you can bring value and engage people. It does not have to be 100-percent related to your product or service, but you can bridge this. How can you help your customer when he is on the move? Remember it's an always-connected third arm! This can be done if you deliver value based on the actual location of mobile of the user; help them find a restaurant, a tourist site, or a retail outlet. Or, give the users value based on their usage or on their lifecycle or help keep people up to date on their daily agenda. People normally use apps for microtasking. Don't overcomplicate the app.

Another and perhaps the most important usage are the games. Games have been very popular since the launch of personal computers, but by making them portable first with Gameboys and Nintendo's and now with all types of smartphones their popularity has exploded. We could say that they are filling the spare time we once had, waiting in line at the supermarket, in the train, waiting for an airplane,… Boredom does not exist anymore. If we have one spare minute it is used to open our smartphone and play a game. In the table below you see an overview of the most popular categories. Gaming is the main category on both smartphones and tablets.

A way to relate to your customers in a creative, fun way is to create games. As I mentioned in the first chapter games are a perfect way to make learning funnier and more effective. With the rise of tablets and smartphone there is now a fantastic vehicle to implement this gamification!

Learning while playing! It is no surprise that education comes at the second spot on the popularity list. Most developers and I include myself; have found a way to combine both education and gaming.

Gaming, entertaining and education might take up nearly 50% of the app space, there are many other possibilities and I personally think that one big opportunity is to use apps as an enhancement of your business or as a research tool. Let people use their phones or apps as an input tool that generate data; like medical parameters. Some pharmaceuticals can greatly benefit from this. They can also remind the patients to take their medication and can have some interaction with them to capture health information. Health and fitness app usage has grown at nearly twice the rate of overall app usage through the first half of 2014, according to Flurry[21].

---

21   http://www.flurry.com/blog/flurry-insights/health-and-fitness-apps-finally-take-fueled-fitness-fanatics

An important point I have to make is that tablets and smartphones are very different, and as a marketer you should understand the difference. Smartphones are part of us; we always have ours with us and don't like to pass it to someone else. It's arguably part of our privacy. Tablets, on the other hand, are more like a smaller lighter notebook typically shared with the whole family and therefore also often used to watch videos, play games, or for education, but less so for micro-task and geolocation-related apps.

Current Active Application Count By Category		
Category	Total	% of Total
Games	260,630	20.32%
Education	132,805	10.36%
Business	120,817	9.42%
Lifestyle	102,714	8.01%
Entertainment	91,574	7.14%
Utilities	66,951	5.22%
Travel	61,673	4.81%
Book	55,387	4.32%
Music	41,574	3.24%
Productivity	36,821	2.87%
Sports	35,051	2.73%
Health & Fitness	35,040	2.73%
Reference	33,034	2.58%
Photo & Video	32,769	2.56%
News	31,199	2.43%
Finance	31,114	2.43%
Food & Drink	27,858	2.17%
Medical	27,082	2.11%
Social Networking	24,280	1.89%
Navigation	16,343	1.27%
Catalogs	8,885	0.69%
Weather	4,833	0.38%
Graphics & Design	1,056	0.08%
Developer Tools	976	0.08%
Video	957	0.07%
Photography	882	0.07%
Healthcare & Fitness	1	0.00%
Tech News	1	0.00%
Total	1,282,307	

Illustration 2.7: App Categories, source Flurry.com

Myth #10: I Need a CRM Tool

I've seen so many companies spending fortunes on creating their own CRM (customer relationship management) tool or implementing seven-figure packages, yet rarely have I seen cases where these CRM tools are giving good results. Why? Because these businesses have an "internal" strategy focusing on the sales reps but not on the *relationship with the customer*. In my view this should not be the focus. Most of the tools do capture a lot of the customer's DNA, his transactions and when a sales rep has visited him with some comments, but what it misses are all the interactions between the customer and you both off-line and online. Did the customer open the e-mail? Did he click on the link and watch the video? Did the customer download the white paper[22]? Did he ask for a quote? Is the prospect ready to be called or visited? Does she want more frequent news?

These are the most valuable pieces of information for a marketer. This information should be used to trigger the communication flows, marketing campaigns and other events like: send a mail, call or visit the prospect, invite her to an event, each prospect at his own pace.

The power lies in combining the captured data with your marketing efforts. Sounds like science fiction or very expensive to implement? You don't have to spend thousands of dollars to build personalized tools. Do not reinvent the wheel and create something from scratch. There are many tools that you can use to do all these things and many more. MailChimp, Aweber or iContact are some of the basic tools you could use, but I strongly recommend to spend a little bit more and use tools like Infusionsoft, or the more expensive Marketo or HubSpot. With $300/month you can already have a deluxe CRM combined with an automated campaign management.

---

22   A white paper is an authoritative report or guide helping readers understand an issue, solve a problem, or make a decision

Automated marketing also means that you can use your sales force more efficiently and effectively. You will need fewer sales people because they will only visit or call customers after they have already been educated with information about the products or services or only when the prospects are ready to buy or to receive extra information. The sales people will also be more effective because they will only visit prospects with a high probability to buy. Their closing rate will be higher and so will their morale!

These tools can really improve your business considerably, but they are only tools. A tool is just an empty box if you don't set it up correctly. Online is harder than offline but if you set it up properly it will help to grow your business considerably on autopilot. With your new marketing mindsets it is now time to learn how to design your online marketing strategy and and how to build the roadmap. In the next chapter I'll guide you step-by-step through the proven methodology that I use with my clients.

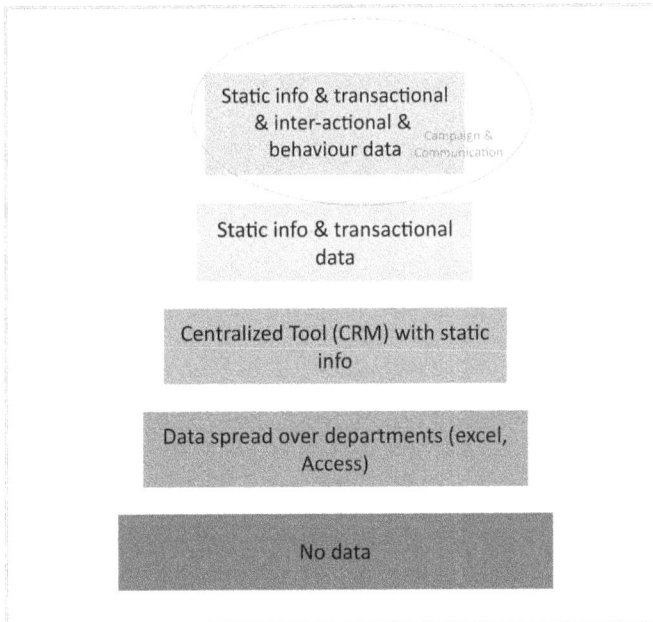

Static info & transactional & inter-actional & behaviour data *Campaign & Communication*

Static info & transactional data

Centralized Tool (CRM) with static info

Data spread over departments (excel, Access)

No data

Illustration 2.8 : phases of CRM's

PART 3

The Online Framework

"The real voyage of discovery consists not in seeking new landscapes but in having new eyes"

Marcel Proust

By now you should have a better view on the impacts of the digitalization on your customers and prospects and how your marketing and sales are being affected. With these new marketing mindsets we are now ready to take advantage of the huge opportunities that online marketing offers and leverage your business to higher spaces.

Your marketing challenge can be divided in two parts: *What you have to do* and *how to do it*.

1. *What you have to do* is what psychologist would call the adaptive challenge. We have *to define the strategy* in order to bring in more customers, or get more sales out of your existing customers. This challenge will differ depending on the product or service you offer. Every business has different customers, competitors and commercial parameters and will have a unique strategy. For the strategy some extra creativity and ingredients will be necessary.

2. *How you have to do it* is the technical challenge. This is more the manual to implement step-by-step what you decided to do. It's like installing software or like building a house. There are some chronological steps to follow.

In this part I'll provide you with a framework that will help you with both challenges. The adaptive challenge or what to do will of course depend on the type of business you have. You can indeed shorten or skip some steps, but nevertheless I strongly believe that it is crucial to have an understanding of the full model and the purpose of each step. Afterwards you can decide how to adapt it for your own business on what you think is optimal for your market.

As you'll read later on one part of the framework is educating the prospect. This is the step that perhaps will differ the most from one business to another. Some parameters that will impact the level of education of a prospects are:

- The urgency people need your product.
  Examples: Is it an urgent problem solver for the need to ship a parcel from A to B; the need to open your locked door, or a medicine to relieve your headache? Or is it a long-term purchase: home automation or buying a house.

- The value and type of the purchase. The higher the value the longer the decision-making process and education phase will be. Buying some sweets on impulse is not the same thing as choosing to pay $1,000 for a course on investing your money.

But be aware that the biggest mistake most marketers make is to try to bypass or combine different steps as this ends up with worse results.

This framework is a the result of my own online experience, working with many clients in different industries, reading hundreds of books, watching dozens of online courses, going to lots of seminars, participating in various masterminds. It is not my objective to cover everything in detail. For more in depth reading, I'll provide you some references of the best books that you can read to complement this one.

The framework has three parts

A. The ABC foundation

This is the crucial prework you have to do properly.

Audience: You identify your ideal niches, try to understand their desires and needs, evaluate the potential and choose one at a time to target. .

Bait: You identify what will attract them into your funnel.

Competitor: You identify the competition and design your USP, unique selling proposition.

B. The six-step funnel: Acquiring your customers or getting from unidentified prospect to customer

1. Traffic: Use various channels to attract your prospects

2. Conversion: Identify your prospect. Here you exchange some first value piece to get your prospect's e-mail

3. Education: The readiness of your prospects to buy from you will vary and the largest part will not be ready from the first time, so you will have to nurture them: educate and motivate them till they are ready to buy from you

4. First-time buyer: This is where your prospect opens his wallet and changes status from prospect into buyer. We will see how to do this and why this is so important.

5. *Selling your core offer:* Steps 1–4 are the acquisition process and in these steps you actually start making money with your core offer.

6. *Maximizing the sales:* Here you try to leverage as much as you can through upselling, cross-selling or down-selling.

The power of this funnel approach is if you design it well and have enough data you will know how much you can afford for Steps 1–4, what we can call *the acquisition phase,* and monetize them in Steps 5 and 6, so that you really can outcompete your competitors.

Once the process works you can finetune it to get even better results and more importantly automate the whole process. This is what I would call the *scaling process*. If set up properly, you can use marketing automation tools lie Infusionsoft to work on autopilot. How to translate this into the tool will be covered in the last chapter of the book.

C. The leverage stage

The top of the pyramid is where you can really leverage your business. Your past customers are always your best next prospects. It's always cheaper to create loyalty than to acquire new ones. But you can also have your customers help you as a new sales channel and use them for social proof and testimonials.

Now it's time for the real stuff and get started to lay the foundations of our model. If a kids wants to learn to read it has to learn the alphabet or what in some languages is called the "ABC". This is also our first and often overlooked basis to build our online marketing strategy.

A stands for Audience

B stands for Bait

C stands for Competition

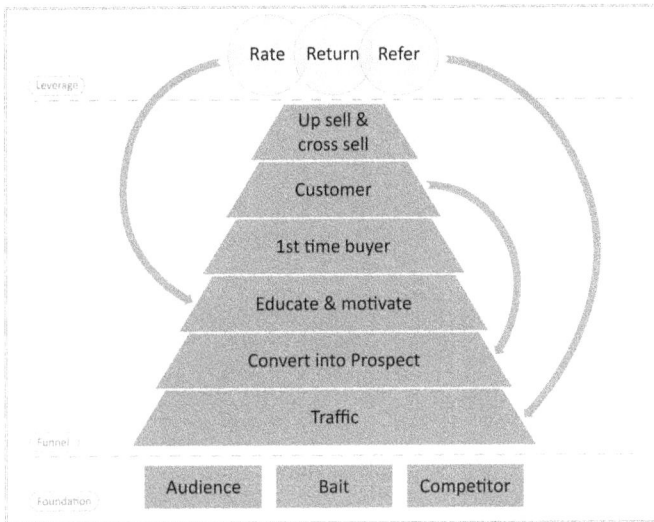

Illustration: The Online Funnel

CHAPTER 3

The ABC Foundation

"It ain't what you don't know that gets you into trouble.
It's what you know for sure that just ain't so"

Mark Twain

Step #1 Define Your Target Audience

Imagine you have a headache and enter a pharmacy to find some medication to relieve your pain.

You have a choice of Aspirin, Ibuprofen, or "Algipain" medicine that says: This pill relieves all possible pains. Would you even consider this last one? Of course not. It's too broad. Even if this medicine has the same chemical composition you would not buy it.

The big companies like Procter & Gamble have applied this for decades and created billion-dollar brands by narrowing their target groups.

Take cosmetics, for example. There is not one type of makeup that will work well for all women. This is definitely not a mass-market product. You want to divide this large market into relatively homogeneous segments of customers, so that you can fully satisfy needs with a different product. In this case, for instance, you may want cosmetics for different skin needs, such as dry, normal, or oily skin. Or, you may want to have ethnic products for African Americans, Asians, Caucasians, and the variations in between. Instead of conducting promotions in all these markets at the same time, you should be addressing them one at a time. Even dry skin can be divided into smaller variables, such as a woman's age, coloring, and daily activities. Even if the composition of most of these cosmetics is fairly similar, packaging them differently and targeting those groups will be the key to success.

This does not mean that you will ignore the other niches, but only that you take one niche at a time. You choose your particular niche, optimize the best way to promote it, and then go on to another niche. This is a difficult exercise, because it takes a lot of patience. You want fast results and are used to the old marketing "numbers game." The more people you reach the more you'll convert. But this hypothesis is purely based on the assumption that the conversion is the same when you target a big audience or a small-niche targeted audience that you understand, know their fears, problems, and how to speak to them. If you were a photographer and had the choice between promoting yourself at a seminar with a thousand people or getting the list of twenty who are getting married this year, what would you choose? I hope you've chosen the latter. This option allows you to focus on their needs, not "photography," but wedding photography, where you can show them your expertise and what you can do, not bothering them with other kinds of photography they might not be interested in. Being "laser-focused" you can adapt the marketing sequence to the end user's interests.

Before online existed and the main direct-response marketing medium was direct mail, the marketers had to do this narrowing exercise. They had to limit the number of targets, because there was a cost linked to them: printing and postage. Paradoxically there were fewer options to segment but the marketer was forced to do a better job at understanding and segmenting.

In fact the narrowing effect has proven to be very successful even in situations that are not so obvious. When a sales area is too large, it is difficult for the salespeople to focus on all the smaller opportunities that may arise. They often get better results in a reduced area than in a larger one, because they can focus in, better understand, and serve their customers.

Narrowing the focus does not mean leaving the other segments behind, not at all.

What you do is choose the best target, be laser-focused, and then start with another one.

But you do this one at a time! Not only will the prospect relate more to your offer but you can also charge more. Think of where the highest tickets are paid: general products or tailor-made ones; general practitioners or specialists?

The exercise of narrowing even further can really be beneficial. Here some examples to help you in better understanding the idea.

Broad	Niche	Sub-niche	Sub-sub-niche
Pets	Dogs	Gun dogs	Golden retriever
Sports	Running	Marathon runners	First-time marathon runners
Photography	Industrial photography	Objects photography	Bottles photography

Finding your Customer Avatar

Finding and prioritizing the niches

How do we come up with different niches and how can we prioritize them?

You might know your product and have an idea of some niches but there is a better way to identify and rank them in a logical way:

Here is a simple framework that will help you with this. On one hand it will help you with the prioritization of your niches but it will also be a guide to better understand your niche, this will then be elaborated further in the next steps of the funnel.

So first I would recommend using the Google Keyword Planner tool.

www.adwords.google.com/KeywordPlanner

Here you can find related words, searches for that keyword, and get an idea of different niches.

Let's imagine I want to sell a course on dog training and target dog owners. So I might type in "golden retriever" into this tool and get following results. (Illustration 3.1) (The results might slightly differ as Google is continuously changing its tools and site.)

Illustration 3.1

So we get ideas for other type of breeds!

Then ideally you make following table and fill scores in the fields based on the research you do.

Niche	# people	# competitors	$ potential (also expanding)	Time frame (decision & cycle)	Opportunity or Problem	Reach	Passion	Ranking
Niche 1	A	B	C	D	E	F	G	H
Niche 2								
Niche 3								

(A)# of people

We try to estimate the total potential niche. The bigger the niche the more potential and possibilities we will have. But we aware that a sub-sub-niche is always better than a broader niche. In this process we will also identify niches that are too small to be targeted.

I'd recommend the following tools to do the exercise:

- Google AdWords Keyword Planner. Here you can evaluate the number of searches a certain keyword gets per month in a specific language and or territory. The example above shows us that there are more searches for rottweiler.

- Facebook: You can simulate an ad and see the number of people that might be interested in your topic.

- You can check the number of tweets that you get for a certain keyword related to your niche.

- Look at your competitor's sites and analyze them. Find out how many visitors they have and their demographics. Some useful tools are:

  - Quantcast.com
  - Alexa.com
  - SEMrush.com

- Are there forums for that niche? Are there magazines on that niche topic?

With all this information give your niche a score between 1 to 10, based on the number of potential buyers you estimated from the research exercises.

(B) Competitors

How many competitors are out there? Do they own the space? It is important that there is some competition, however, it should not be saturated. Look at their websites, the number of visitors. What keywords are bringing people to your competitor's website?

Look at the AdWords and their bid prices. The higher the prices, the more competition but this also means that there is money to be made.

(C) Potential money

Analyze the AdWords bidding prices. You should look at the offers of the competitors. These is an excellent indicator whether people are making money on them. The higher the bids, the more money can be made, but the negative side is that there is also more competition for these. So you'll have to pay more to get them too.

(D) Time frame

How actively is your prospect looking for a solution? Is the need very urgent.

Is he waiting for the ambulance or is it something that can wait? Do you need to educate them a lot; do you have to show him his problem? An important point here is that you should avoid educating the market yourself. I have seen many companies failing because they had to open the way. Of course you have the iPads and iPhones, but as a general rule if there is no competition, the prospect's need has to be educated. Be very careful!

(E)Is it an opportunity or a problem that we will solve

If your product or service solves the problem there might be no business afterwards, unless it is a recurrent problem. Typically you will see that problems are more time critical, however having a solution to answer an opportunity might be a lot better. People buy services or products to pave the way to their dreams. With opportunities you can always expand *and* have transformational changes. In most instances solutions for opportunities can be sold at a higher ticket.

(F)Reach

How easily can I reach my audience?
Can you reach them on one of the five online traffic highways:

- Google

- Facebook

- Youtube

- Amazon

- iTunes (Podcast, Apps)

What keywords can I bid on and what will be the total volume?
Can I target them on Facebook? How many?
Do I have an e-mail list? Can I buy/rent one?
Is it easy to get the data of potential contacts? B2B data is normally easier to get.

(G)Passion

How much do I like this niche or what affinity do I have with this niche? This is the only subjective parameter, but it can be an important one. If you are passionate about something you will be eager to learn more about it and will also communicate better with your niche.

(H)Ranking

When you score the seven parameters, you add them, and the final score is the niche score.
If you do this for all the niches you'll get a ranking that you can use as prioritization.

Starting with existing customers
If you already have customers, you have gold in your hands that you might easily overlook.
   Do some data mining to identify your best segments.

I usually recommend starting with two data mining exercises:

1) 80/20

Here we look at the 20 percent customers that are bringing 80 percent of the

- profit
- revenue
- growth

and look to see if there are some commonalities.

If your business is a Busines-to-Business (B2B), you might analyze these top groups and try to find the main industries, the size of the company or top location and define your target company profile
If your business is Business-to Consumer (B2C) look at the data you have: If you don't have these, so called DNA data (gender, age, marital status, number of children, hobbies, education level, income level, type of employment) you might consider mailing them a survey. SurveyMonkey.com is a great tool to do this. What you are doing is what we now call: creating your customer's "avatar." Basically, this means identifying the commonalities of your target market or ideal client and establishing a simplified image of this person.

2.) RFM

This methodology is the old solid way to get your best customers. You will rank them based on three parameters

- Recency (R): last buying data

- Frequency (F): how often did they buy

- Monetary Value (M): how much did they spend in total
  You take the database and divide it into percentiles of 10 percent (so group them in 10) and the top receives 10 points, second tier 9 points, third tier 8 points and so on. You do this exercise for each parameter. And then you add the three scores together. The highest points are the ones to analyze. These are your best customers. Ideally you should focus on this niche.

Step #2 Define the "bait" for your audience

Now that you have identified your FIRST niche, you should focus ONLY on that one. Notice that I say FIRST niche, indeed this will ideally be a SEQUENTIAL process whereby you pick various niches and do the exercise over and over again. But as with most things in life, success will come if you FOCUS your full attention and energy on this ideal niche. The next step is now to understand your ideal niche's desired end result. What you should do is try to put yourself in the shoes of your ideal prospect. "The secret of the best fishermen is not to know how to have and use the best fishing gear, it is to think like the fishes." Try to make an avatar. You might even give him or her a face and name. You will see that everything will be easier. You'll be able to understand your prospect better and you will not speak to a group but to an individual as if it were on a one-to-one basis!

Begin with the end in mind: what is the desired end result and find out the path to arrive to that result. Can you identify different milestones?

These milestones will usually be the steps in resolving obstacles or problems that one might encounter in achieving the end result. In other words, each step means bringing the prospect closer to their desired end result.

You might think, "How do I find these steps?" It's comparable to a chess master who knows his end goal: "checkmate king" and goes backward to understand the steps in achieving this.

The best way to find this out for your prospect is putting yourself in his shoes; be the fish instead of the fisherman. Ideal ways to understand your prospect and what is going on in his mind is going to YouTube, Facebook, and looking at posts and videos. Sign up on forums and see what your niche prospects are talking about asking. Do a search on Twitter and find the burning topics and questions. Look what your competitor is offering.

What products are being sold on Amazon; look at the comments.

The better you understand your target audience and their objectives, the better you will be able to map out their journey. You have to go as deep as you can to know what the conversations are that they are having in their mind.

If you have them, survey some of your best customers or some prospects. Organize a face-to-face appointment or call them, otherwise you can do an online survey with Surveymonkey. Then expand this "core" information to other topics that support this core information. Ideally you should identify the top topics for your niche. This will be important for the next steps in our funnel. The better you know your target niche, the better you can compel them and speak to them in order to dominate that niche!

The objective is really to lay the foundation for all your next marketing and sales activities.

Once you have identified the various milestones, identify how to help your prospects to move closer to the first milestone. You will create the "bait," "bribe" or lead magnet, as some call it. These are valuable pieces of information or items that we will give for free. This can be:

information, a test, results of a questionnaire, a cheat sheet with key steps, a price calculation, a framework. They can be given in various formats such as a PDF, audio, podcast, a video, membership only website. But you can also give free software. This generally works very well. Some lead magnets or bait is better than others. In order to be successful, your lead magnet should have the following characteristics:

1. It should be easily consumable and give immediate gratification

2. It should be very specific to help your prospect reaching his first milestone

3. It should also have a high-perceived value.

4. Ideally it should be incomplete.

1. Immediate gratification and easily consumable: The prospect does not know you and will not want to spend too much time to consume your bait. Bear in mind that his time is even as valuable as his money. So the key here is to develop something that can be read, watched, or used quickly, in fifteen minutes or less, but at the same time will give the prospect great value. Think about TED[23] talks: great value and . . . less than fifteen minutes.
    Most people will not consume your bait, but those that will are your best prospects.
    Books or minicourses for example are not good lead magnets. The value can be enormous, but very few prospects will consume the information. Give them rather a summary or quick report.

2. Very specific information or help. Don't give theory away. Your bait should be of direct practical value, it should really help the prospect get closer to the end result. Moving your prospect closer is the key to success. Get the prospect moving, and if he sees the value,

---

23   TED: (Technology, Entertainment, Design) is a global set of conferences of 15 minutes owned by the private non-profit Sapling Foundation, under the slogan: "Ideas Worth Spreading".

he'll be open for more. One of the biggest mistakes is to make the information not specific enough and fall into the "generalization" trap. Too often sites give away a general report or white paper about a topic. Your piece should answer a specific question.

3. High value. The information or item you give away should be of the highest value. You should not give "crappy" stuff away. The perception of the customer of your value to him will be based on this first interaction. If you give great value, he'll think, "If this great value is for free, the paid value will have to be excellent!" Many marketers have problems in giving great stuff away, but this is what you have to do. This is the way to get through the attention filters. We are living in a freemium economy. The bait should also not be seen as a "bait" or "bribe" as such. People are way too sophisticated these days. If they perceive your "value piece" is a bait or bribe, they will quit immediately. The awesome marketer Dean Jackson came up with a great analogy and talks about cheese and whiskers. You need a "more cheese, less whiskers" approach at lead generation. A mouse is programmed to sniff out and follow the cheese. However, if it sees just the whiskers of the cat—the barest notice—the mouse will run away. We react like these mice, when we see the least sign of advertising, we are repelled instead of compelled. We have to make our first piece so valuable that it is perceived as 100% pure value for the prospect. So ideally don't brand it!

4. Incomplete: After the prospects consume the lead magnet, they should have the "WOW" effect, but the lead magnet should not resolve all their steps to get to the desired result. It should open the way to the next step, so that they'll want more of what you gave them.

Cheese versus Cats

Step #3 Analyze your Competition and Define your Unique Selling Proposition (USP)

Now we will analyze in detail our competition and define how we can be better—and unique.

Often people see innovations and new developments as ideas coming "out of the blue." Someone wakes up and has a great idea and implements it, but the majority of the big innovations are improvements of already existing products or services.

Examples:

Creating new markets is so difficult. In my professional life I've seen so many companies that thought they had a good innovative idea and wanted to be the first on the market. Most of them, not to say all of them FAILED. It is important to look at what the competitors are doing and analyzing what is working, if people are spending money on their services or products. If some services do not work there is a huge risk that if you launch them, they won't either. A huge mistake is for instance to rely on some market study where people are asked their intentions. Most of the people would like to change or quit their jobs, but how many do? How many people want to lose weight and even show the intention to start to go to the gym in January, but how many follow through?

Don't be the first, but be the best. So what you have to do is analyze what is working for your competitors and what isn't. Copy and improve what works! The big advantage today is that we have so much competitors' data available: the best keywords, the campaigns that are working for them. What kind of visitors they have. . .

This analysis will also help refine the previous steps.

What is also key here is to really find how you can differentiate your content in a better, more appealing way. How can you add more value than your competitor is giving?

So the practical way to do this is:

- Find out who your competitors are with a very simple search in Google: Enter your URL, *mycompany.com*, or the one of a known competitor instead of mycompany.com

- Analyze the website's offers. Subscribe to its newsletter. Be a customer of your competitor.

- Use the tools

  - www.alexa.com

  - www.semrush.com

  - www.quantcast.com

  - www.compete.com

To find out more about their visitors and traffic, you can see which keywords people are typing to get to their website; what paid keywords they are bidding on.

All this information is crucial to set the foundation for the following steps. Most often people jump into setting up a funnel without doing their homework properly. If you have defined your niche, know the desired end result, the stepping-stones to achieve it, defined the bait to compel your prospects so that they'll identify themselves, know how you can differentiate yourself, you are ready to set up your funnel.

CHAPTER 4

Traffic building

"The uninformed would be staggered to know the amount of work involved in a single ad. Weeks of work sometimes. The ad seems so simple, and it must be simple to appeal to simple people. But back of that ad may lie reams of data, volumes of information, months of research"

Claude C. Hopkins, Scientific Advertising

So how do you attract your potential customers in a world of clutter and so much distraction?

Here is where we start using all the detailed research we did in the last chapter: By now we have defined our ideal niche; we know what their end goal is and what could be the first step in order to accomplish that end goal. Now we need to get their attention or in Internet marketing terms we need to create traffic. For this, we will not use the classical "branding" methods or "broad"-casting, that has been so misused by corporate companies. Instead we'll use direct-response marketing (DRM).

DRM evokes an immediate response and entices individuals to act upon our ads or teasers. DRM has immediate cause-and-effect results that you can track. You can test, optimize, and scale. You set up the funnel, and always split test with—ideally—two options. When you have enough data—statistically significant—you pick the best one and create a new piece that you split test against the "winner." This way you'll always improve your results!

So let's go back to creating a way through the clutter. Some studies say that we are exposed to some five thousand ads each day, of which we remember nearly none. So how will you win the battle and get someone's attention?

What you have to do is look at advertisements from another point of view. You know by now what the questions are in your prospect's mind. You have to give them a piece of the answer. It has to be tailor-made to their needs and related to the outcome you are going to sell him in a later stage.

You need to make "educational ads." Today we call them *native ads*. What this means is that the ads are not seen as sales pitches, but as valuable information. In the newspaper and magazine worlds this has been called an *infomercial*. You want to show your prospects only "the cheese" and not the "whiskers." Therefore it is important that you don't stuff your ads with logos or promises that seem unrealistic. No branded ads or logos that trigger the filters. Instead, the buyers are looking for "cheese," or information that can be considered of value. In the off-line world it is very similar with direct mailings. If the envelope looks like a commercial letter, it will go in the pile for the trash can. The ad should be something they are really interested in, something really compelling. It's compelling, because you cannot *not* pay attention. For example when you're driving by an car accident, and all the people in front of you are slowing down and people are screaming, "Idiots! Morons!" They have to gawk at the car accident, to see if anyone's hurt, dead, maimed, whatever. And it's kind of morbid curiosity, and people get angry because there's a big, huge line. Then, the moment you drive by it, you slow down, and you become one of those same people that you're complaining about! The big mistake that businesses often make is they think that compelling prospects to call you means getting your name out there, getting people to know who your business is. And that's not it at all. The very best thing you can do is put your own ego aside and focus only on what your prospects really want . . . without even any mention of YOU or your business up front.

Robert Collier[24] talked about entering the conversation that's already going on in your prospect's mind. Once you understand your target market, you're not going to try and convince them to do something; you're going to get their attention by showing them how to do something

---

24   Robert Collier (April 19, 1885 in St. Louis, Missouri - 1950) was an American author of self-help, and New Thought metaphysical books in the 20th century

that's already on their mind. They're already thinking about how to do this. This is not new science, however in this world of clutter and overly distracted people and online, where everything is anonymous, it's only more relevant than it was in the past.

With this basic principle in mind, I'll now cover the various channels that you can use and how to use them.

As I explained in the chapter about the marketing myths, you don't have to build the traffic from scratch. This is one of the main error people make. They want to build their traffic completely themselves. This takes lots of effort and is time-consuming. It's like wanting to build your own railway infrastructure while high-speed trains pass by. This infrastructure is already is there for you. The five main high-speed online channels are Google, Amazon, iTunes, YouTube, and Facebook. There are also other smaller ones out there but let's concentrate on the big five.

What you now have to do is understand "*how to use them properly.*"

It's important to view traffic from the "prospect's point of view," and understand the prospect's mindset when he is consuming information through the channel.

When you have a burning problem you will look for a solution as soon as possible. In the past you might have used the Yellow Pages, but today most likely you'll type your search into Google. This is a completely different way of consuming the information than if you are reading some posts on Facebook

When you are querying on Google you are "proactively" looking for something at that exact moment, and for an advertiser the task is to compel that person more than the others. Your prospect is looking for a solution. Compare that with getting the attention of someone reading something that has nothing to do with your service or offer. In the second case you have to disrupt the train of thought and be very clever to get their attention. Here you are targeting a potential prospect that is thinking or doing something else! To choose and understand better the different types of traffic, I've divided the channels into five main categories:

1) *Search:* Here the prospect is actively looking for something matching "your" solution

2) *Interrupt:* Here the prospect is not looking for your solution, but you've targeted the ones that might be interested and you are trying to interrupt them with your message.

3) *Informational:* The prospect is reading related information to your offer. This can be in online press releases or specialized press.

4) *Direct Contact:* Here you are directly contacting your prospects, they might be interested or not at this stage.

5) *Indirect Contact:* Partners and affiliates: A third party that already has interaction with them is contacting your ideal prospects.

The order I'm listing these is important. Because it is a guideline on how you should progress. Search is a smaller group, but definitely the most sophisticated or proactive prospects and they are more likely to convert into buyers. They are already looking for a solution. They represent only fraction of the total addressable market. The "fishing pond" of prospects is a lot bigger. Most of them "might be interested" but do not have an urgent need yet to buy your product. They also might have a longer decision-making process. Therefore it's important first to learn how to attract and convert the proactive prospects before starting with the others. We are interrupting them in a state that might not be very optimal. We'll analyze the 3 types of interruption in detail.

The last category, the partners, is often forgotten but of extreme importance. It should definitely be leveraged only when you have tested and optimized the other channels. Your whole funnel should be well in place, so that you can show your partners some results before they start contacting their customers. That will increase the likelihood that they actively promote your products or services.

Let's take a deep dive into all these various traffic modes.

1. Search

When someone types a keyword in Google, it means that person is actively looking for an answer to a question. Search terms can be more or less detailed. You can just look for a general term, such as "water," or be more specific, such as "bottle of water" or even more exact such as, "where can I buy a bottle of water?" Today, more and more people are putting complete questions into the search engine. A general word can be anything from "shortage of water" to "purified water." For example, "I want to buy a bottle of water. Where can I find it?" is a very long search and only a few people will ask such a long question. Yet this person is much better qualified, because he or she is looking for something specific. The same is true for specific brands: When people put in more detail for search terms, they are already thinking about specific needs. This is very important to understand, because you will have to design your ad copy and *landing page*—the page they will land on after clicking on your ad—accordingly.

Search can be divided into two main categories: paid search and free or organic, search. It's important to clarify some terminology: SEA—Search Engine Advertising—is the function of paying for certain keywords and being ranked for those in the "paid section" of the search results and SEO—Search Engine Optimization, this means improving your organic search ranking.

A lot of myths exist about organic search and SEO. Most of the searches happen on Google. You type a keyword and get a search result. The results that are not located on the top or on the right side of the page are the highest organic search results. Google ranks these results based on a "secret" algorithm, which is changed quite often and always remains a black box. Google does this to counter those who know how to manipulate these results. This has happened a lot in the past. Some tried to spin content with a lot of keywords to rank artificially higher. If Google allowed this, the search results would not be optimal and people might leave Google for other search engines. That's why Google tries to deliver the best result it can, both on the free (organic) as on the paid results for any given query. In the last few years Google has made major changes in its search algorithm to penalize these websites that were trying to game the rankings.

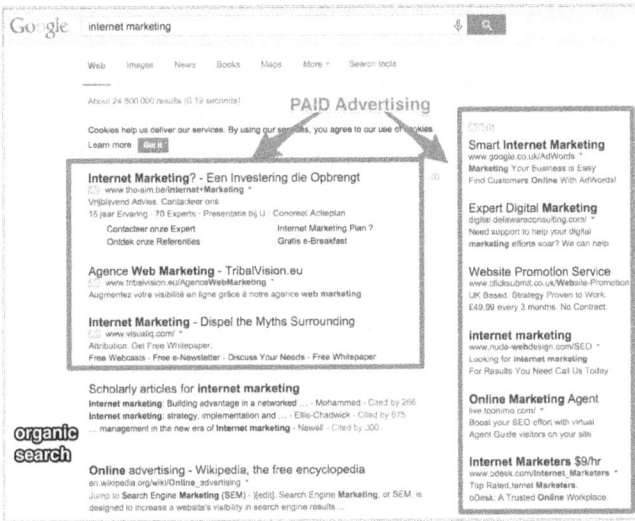

Illustration 4.1: Paid versus Organic Advertising

The first update was Panda, which looked at a whole website for quality, statistics elements, and user experience. The second was the Penguin update: Google looked at all those cheating links that were received through content farms[25] and linking to sites. Now, Google started giving negative points for this. All links from these pirate sites decreased a website's total score and ranking on keyword results.

Now let's dive into the two types of traffic building techniques through search:

a. Paid

The concept of paid search or SEA is simple: it's a bidding system where you pay to get your ad in the search results for a certain keyword and

---

25   a content farm is a company that employs large numbers of freelance writers
      to generate large amounts of textual content designed to satisfy algorithms of
      search engines

only pay when someone clicks on your ad. Based on your daily budget your ad will appear till the budget is depleted. The system is a little bit more complex than just the highest bidder gets the best rankings. It's based on an algorithm of Google. When someone clicks on your ad you pay—also known as PPC, pay per click. Your cost per click—CPC—will again depend on Google's algorithm. A good ratio is a 2 percent click-through rate—CTR—on your ads. This means that for every fifty times your ad is shown someone clicks on your ad.

Another payment system, that is less used is CPM—cost per mille. Here Google charges you an amount that you bid to show your ad a thousand times. I would not recommend starting with this. This can be used to lower your costs once you have a very high CTR.

So how does the Google algorithm work? To understand this, look at the example below. Four advertisers are bidding on the same keyword. Let's say it's "internet marketing." Look at the table below to see the various bids for each advertiser. So Advertiser 1 bids $10, Advertiser 2 bids $6, Advertiser 3 bids $4, and Advertiser 4 bids $2. Intuitively you should think that Advertiser 1 will always show up on the first place because they are bidding the most.

	Max Bid	CTR	Potential income for Google per 100 impressions	Best for Google
Advertiser 1	$10	1%	$10	4
Advertiser 2	$6	8%	$48	1
Advertiser 3	$4	3%	$12	3
Advertiser 4	$2	10%	$20	2

This is however NOT how the system works. Google has created a Quality Score in order to improve the relevance and optimize its ad income.

Imagine that Advertiser 1, who bids $10 gets only 1 percent clicks, and Advertiser 2, who bids $6, gets 8 percent clicks when the ad is shown; Google will make $10 for Advertiser 1 and $48 for Advertiser 2 on every 100 times they are shown. Therefore Google will rank Advertiser 2 higher than Advertiser 1, even if Advertiser 1 is bidding more. Google has all interest to place Advertiser 2 above Advertiser 1 in the search results. Google will not only use the CTR to rank the different advertisers, but also includes some relevancy parameters in its algorithm. The main parameter that will be included with the bid price is called the Quality Score. In the table below you see some fictive examples. Google will multiply the Quality Score and get an Ad Rank that will define the final position. (Ad Rank = max bid * Quality Score) .

	Max Bid	Quality Score	Ad Rank	Position	Actual Cost
Advertiser 2	$6	8	48	1	$2,5
Advertiser 4	$2	10	20	2	$1,2
Advertiser 3	$4	3	12	3	$3,3
Advertiser 1	$10	1	10	4 (or not ranked)	

You see that for this example even if Advertiser 1 is bidding the most—five times what Advertiser 4 is bidding—his ads might not even appear.

Important to note is that often the actual cost per click and the max bid per click will not be the same. You may in fact bid $6 but usually in the end pay less. Google will discount your CPC down just to appear above your competitor with $0.01 more. The actual formula to determine this is: actual CPC = Ad Rank to Beat / (your quality score +$0.01)

For Advertiser 2 this is: 20/ (8 + 0.01) = $2,5

For Advertiser 3 this is: 10/ (3 + 0,01) = $3,3

In our example you see that Advertiser 2 is paying less than Advertiser 3 and has 2 positions higher even though he is bidding $6 compared to $4 for Advertiser 3.

It might seem a bit complicated but I wanted to explain this to stress the importance of the Quality Score, hence the CTR. Because improving your CTR you'll end up paying less—while getting more clicks!

How do you achieve this?

Therefore two key factors are crucial:

- Thorough keyword analysis
- Compelling ad copy based on the keywords

I see many companies; even SEO managers limit themselves to too few keywords, mostly "broad" terms. They should also focus on phrase match and exact match. I'll explain them here below:

1) Broad match

    Broad match means anytime someone types in a keyword phrase that includes that keyword. If your keyword is more than one word, it will be independent of the other.

    For example, if you bid for the keyword: *dog training*, you will always be bidding whenever someone uses a phrase that includes both words "dog" and "training" no matter how it is used. If someone keys in "best *training* for a *dog*" you will be bidding for that phrase.

2) Phrase match: [26]

    With phrase match, you will be bidding whenever some types in a keyword phrase that contains all your keywords, but they'll have to be in the right order. In our example "dog training," the keyword phrase has to include dog training in that order and not separated. So it would not work for: "best *training* for a *dog*" but it would work for "best **dog training**."

3) Exact match:

    Exact match is when your keywords match exactly with the keyword phrase being searched. In our example only when [*dog training*] is typed in exactly will your ad show up.

---

26   in Google AdWords you will have to put quotation marks around the keyword to define phrase match: "keyword" and brackets to define exact match: [keyword]

Finally you also have to define the words you absolutely want to exclude. For example, if you are giving a course on dog training, you may want to exclude the searches for "free courses". Therefore you should exclude the word "free" from all the searches. You need to understand there are many keywords and I suggest most companies come up with a thousand keywords! Start with the ones that you think are really linked to your product or service and exclude the ones that are not.

After you have identified hundred or more good keywords the next part is to create compelling ad copy that will improve your CTR. Your Ad copy will directly impact your click rate and conversion. My advice is to arrange similar keywords into ad groups. Ad groups will group all the keywords that will have the same ad copy. Now you can test different copy on all those keywords in the ad group.

Testing is all-important. The best framework for ads is a headline followed by three lines, with the last line being your URL. The headline must have your keyword, because it relates to the person's search. The second line should always give some benefit, and the third line should give some feature or offer that motivates people to click on the link. This is the first step toward conversion.

> **How to better train your dog?**
>
> **Watch the free video**
>
> **7 tips to have an obedient pet**
>
> **www.dogtraining.com**

Illustration 4.2 : An Example of a good AdCopy

What do you do when you have thousands of keywords with different copy? The expert on this is Perry Marshall, who wrote an excellent book on paid advertising called *The Ultimate Guide to Google AdWords*.[27]

---

27   Ultimate Guide to Google AdWords: How to Access 1 Billion People in 10
      Minutes, by Perry Marshall, Mike Rhodes,Bryan Todd

It's definitely the best book on this topic. One of his methods is the "peel-and-stick." You have all those keywords separated into ad groups. When one keyword is doing very well in an ad group, take that keyword from that ad and create a new ad group with this word in the headline. Typically what you will see is that your click-through rate on this newly created ad will increase

Two last notes on SEA:

Your results might not be optimal when you start and this might be because Google puts up artificial barriers for new advertisers. But if you do your work properly you'll see the benefits.

And don't be obsessed with your ranking. It's not always the best to have the number one position. You might get the most clicks, including many impulse clicks with low conversion.

b. Organic Search

Once you have your initial paid search results and know which keywords are the most valuable and convert into paying customers you can selectively choose keywords to optimize organically.

Sometimes it is possible that some keywords are so expensive due to the high competition and that you are not getting a positive return on investment (ROI) out of them, so you'll have to invest in getting the intelligence to optimize your funnel and then start concentrating on SEO traffic to make this a winner. How does Google work and what can you do to get some positive results for SEO?

The Google algorithm is a black box that changes continuously and it might seem mysterious how Google ranks one or another webpage. However it can be boiled down to two parameters that are:

- On-site optimization: everything you can do on your site

- Off-site optimization: all activities outside your site

On site is making sure that your website is properly designed and that it is easy for search engines to find and index you, making proper use of the most important keywords—the ones your customers are using when searching for your product or service.

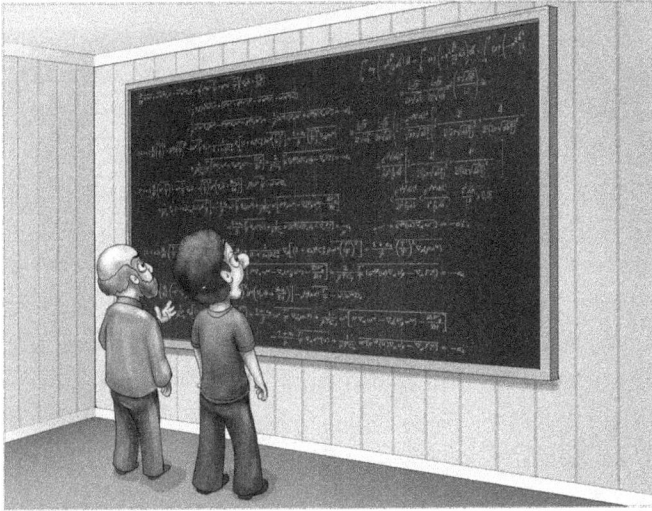

The Google Algorithm

Use the Google Webmaster Tools to make sure that your pages are indexed: www.google.com/webmasters/tools. The hard truth however is that having a search engine friendly site will not increase your rankings, it will only avoid being degraded.

Make sure your content is well designed around your major keywords. These will tell the search engines what your site is about. You should have found these keywords during your SEA activities. These keywords should appear in your titles, subtitles, and content.

But the single most effective approach is off-site optimization: the links that your website receives from other sites. But not all links are equal. Google rates those links based on the importance of the other sites "page rank." You can see it as a voting system where the higher the ranking of the page that links into your website, the more "points" or "link juice" you receive. This ranking is known as PageRank (PR). This goes from 0 to 10. These rankings change, but normally PR 10 (example, Google itself or usa.gov) is for only a dozen sites and PR 9 (example, W3.org, youtube.com, bbc.com) around 144 sites. The higher the PR of an inbound link the more it will count for Google. The link itself is not the only important piece; the "visible keyword" in the link that is called the "anchor text" is of crucial importance. This is what Google will take into account. If you have a site about salmon fishing it is not enough that some other websites link into you, you need them to have your "keyword", here "salmon fishing" in the link. Now Google will give you points on that specific keyword, because it now knows that your page is specifically about salmon fishing. The best way to improve these rankings is deciding what keywords you want to rank for. Then you start creating content around these topics. You can do this yourself or be a content curator, meaning that you act like a museum: You don't have to be the painter, but you bring all nice paintings under one roof, or on a page. It's important but time-consuming work, but in the long run it will give results.

Do not only improve your SEO for Google, the second biggest search engine YouTube is easier to rank for. Even if the number of videos produced and posted on YouTube every day is skyrocketing, comparatively they are still very small compared to all other content produced, and the interesting part is that it is still possible—depending on your keywords—to rank quickly in the top positions for YouTube. On top of that is a side benefit to it. Google owns YouTube and loves videos if your "topic" is appropriate for it. Therefore you'll often see a number of videos in its top ten search results. For example, at the time of writing this book, if you type in "how to fish salmon" four of the top ten results are videos (see below). The good, or bad thing, is that YouTube still cannot identify what your video is about, so you'll have to tell them. This is done in your title, tag's description. Place as many keywords as you can, but do some research before!

Bear in mind SEO takes time and that you'll not see results quickly. You cannot create content and build links hoping that in six months you will rank high on the search for keywords. I'm not saying that you shouldn't work on this, but it is time-consuming—meaning it will also cost money—and you are not sure how Google might update its algorithm. However, as you'll see in the education phase of your funnel, you'll have to create content, so why not use it for SEO purposes! Try to balance organic traffic with SEA. Paid traffic will give you the speed!

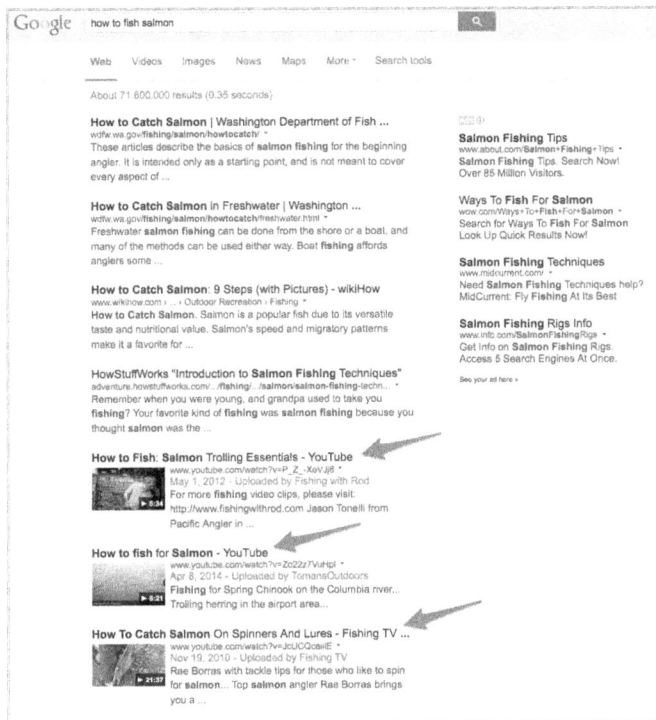

Illustration 4.3

C. The other "search engines"

Marketers often forget that there are other search engines that they can use in addition to Google. And I don't mean Bing or Yahoo! These you can target from your AdWords account. There are other platforms where millions of people are searching every day. Heard of the App Store of Apple, Google Play, or Amazon? More than five hundred million people are registered—most with their credit cards on the App Store and more than two hundred million are buying on Amazon! Not bad if you can tap into those channels?

Do you know that anyone can sell products on Amazon? Amazon has created an amazing platform that not only allows you to market your product but even will collect the money and even has logistic services, to do the picking, and shipping to your customer.

Same with the App Store or Google Play. Make an app and sell it on their platform. I've personally built a living selling apps on the App Store.

But there are other ways to use these engines and leverage their traffic power:On Amazon you can write an e-book for Kindle on your topic—keyword! When people are looking for your keyword you are in the ranking. You can either sell at a low price or give your book away and use it as a platform. Inside your e-book you can now send the readers to your website and enter your funnel! Great lead generation!

On the App Store you can do the same with a free app. Then motivate your users to register for some extra tools or information. You get the users' e-mail and have them entering your funnel! The advantage of the apps is that you can even do push notification, to communicate with them without knowing their e-mail. If someone allows you to send messages out of your app you can then send them messages based on some behavior, on some specific moments or you can broadcast some messages, just as if you would send an email.

Podcasting is another easy way to get on the search engines. You can put a podcast inside iTunes, so people can find you with the right keyword and this can be a source of your growing traffic. The same thing happens with Apple Newsstand. You can create a free magazine that can be the first platform for your funnel. These are all nice opportunities that very few companies use.

Search is the best way to start your traffic and to allow you to set up your funnel, but search will only give you a fraction of the potential customers: only those that are already proactively looking for a solution to their problem. To tap into the bigger pond of all those that are not actively searching you have to interrupt them.

2. Interrupt

Search traffic is a fantastic way to get new prospects into your funnel. In fact it is a dream for marketers. People are searching for a solution and you can put yourself in front of them with your solution. On top of that it is very constant. If you design it well, you guarantee a continuous stable flow of traffic. That's why I personally think it's the best traffic you can start with. The caveat with Search traffic is that it is limited. If only fifty people are searching for your keyword per day, your maximal potential is fifty new prospects/day, assuming they all are new. Is this the only fishing pond you can fish from? Generally speaking search only accounts between 5 and 30 percent of the total potential. So how can you leverage and tap into the others that are not actively searching but may be interested, your "sleeping" prospects. So you'll have to wake them up and get their attention! Be aware that this is more difficult, because you are going to disrupt their train of thought and really interrupt them. Interrupting is a big word. There are different levels of interruption. The likelihood of getting people's attention will increase if: a) your prospect is open for some interruption, and b) if the teaser you use is compelling.

It is crucial to acknowledge this. So when are people "relaxed" and open for new suggestions? In the off-line world when people are rushing to arrive on time at their work your chances are very small. Think of the ads you remember after your last journey. But if you are at the movies, watching television or reading your newspaper at a Starbucks your state of thoughts is completely different and you will more likely be in a relaxed state and open for novelty, if the interruption is appealing or something that interests you. In the online world there is a kind of Starbucks where people are "hanging out," passing their time when bored: Facebook. And what about YouTube: the new television. These places are ideal to interrupt because people are in a relaxed state of mind when they are consuming content. In fact they are looking for interesting stuff. Facebook is their newspaper and YouTube is their television on demand. The interrupted people might not be proactively searching for your solution, but it's up to you to choose whom to interrupt. You can and should target them based on their interests and sociodemographics as well as on topics they are looking for. Blogs are the new specialized magazines, so if your topic is related to the blog's topic, chances are they might be interested. What about someone reading a blog on black-and-white photography, wouldn't they likely be interested in the new gear that Nikon or Canon is launching?

The first rule is to target the right people and the second rule is that you have to attract your prospects in a compelling way!

In this "new" connected world of easy distraction, people are very difficult to attract because of their "ads" filters. Some innate filters will try to block everything that seems like an ad. This is even more important than with AdWords, but so many companies overlook this.

So don't show your whiskers to your prospects, only the cheese!

In this disruptive advertising model there are three channels:

- Social media

- Blogs and specialized websites

- Apps

Social Media

I still believe that social media is the best of the three because of the reach and the targeting possibilities. Let's be clear that I don't mean social media in the context some "social media gurus" would proscribe it. The objective is definitely NOT to get shares or likes, these will be byproducts, and we'll discuss this in a later stage, when we tackle the ratings and reviews. The objective is to FIND the right people and compel them to get OUT of the social media context and enter your landing page and your funnel. You put $1 into advertising and get a multiple out of it! Likes and tweets have no real monetary value, your sales funnel does!

You have various options to choose from in social media but I would concentrate on Facebook and YouTube, and if your market is B2B, LinkedIn might also be a good option. Facebook has more than 1.3 billion users and 1 billion connecting on their mobiles. Nearly two-thirds of the online population is on Facebook. In developed countries you might even say that 75 percent is on Facebook.

Here some other interesting figures about Facebook:

- 76 percent of the total user base looks at Facebook once a day

- Average time per visit is twenty minutes.

- Average daily likes are 4.5 billion: This is four times a day per person.

- 50 million fan book pages.

And advertising on Facebook has become even better than last year. In the past you could only advertise on the right side of the Facebook News Feeds. But the click through was relatively low, less than 1 percent and sometimes closer to 0.1 percent. Now they allow you to be placed inside the news on the left-hand side, like the "infomercials" in between all the posts of your "trusted" friends. This is a subliminal way to advertise, if your ad is not perceived as an ad but as content—hence the native ad name. Now, the mouse does not see the cat, it sees only cheese and your target will click on it. That's what you are doing: Enticing the readers with cheese. The rate on these News Feeds is twenty to forty times higher than the traditional ads on the right-hand side. This is amazing, especially since you can laser target.

Some parameters you can use to target your niche include:

- Country, age range, and gender of the target audience
- Precise interest categories
- People with children of different ages.
- People on different types of devices, such as only those using Android or Apple's iOS.[28]
- Users who are already connected to your friends
- Those who are interested in a certain page(s) or those who are fans of your competitors. This is really huge and can be a treasure.
- By education, language, relationship status, and workplace

But there is even more power if you use the Power Editor of Facebook. Here you can even create custom audiences. You can upload a list of prospects; these can be a list that you bought, your own lost customers, or old prospects. If Facebook matches the e-mails or phone numbers, you can target them with your ads! This can even be used as another way of communicating with your customers, as we'll see in the education phase. Besides sending them e-mails, you can now also appear in the newsfeeds of your customers.

---

28   I've personally used this a lot to sell apps and get top rankings in local markets!

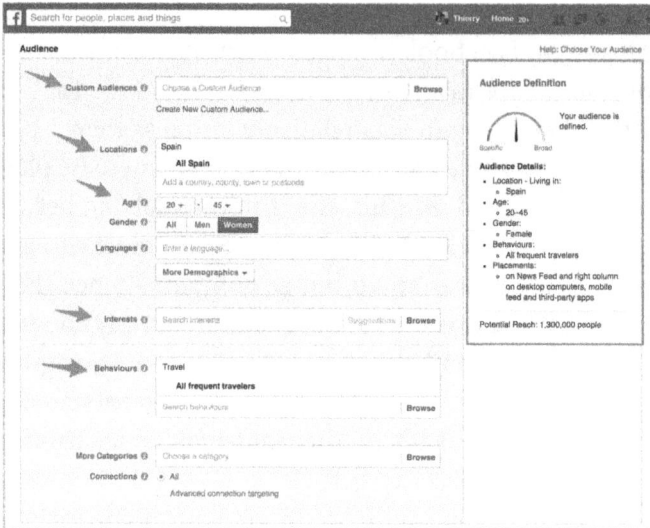

Illustration 4.4 : Example of Facebook Targeting

But there is even more gold inside Facebook. You can now also create an audience with similar profiles than your uploaded list:

1. Upload your customers into the Power Editor.

2. Facebook looks for matching phone numbers or e-mails and creates a customer audience.

3. You now ask to create an "alike" audience.

Besides getting prospects in your funnel, there are other—additional— benefits with these ads, FaceBook calls them promoted News Feeds. Some people will also "like" or "share" your post and this will be visible on their friends' pages as trusted news.

The cost per clicks will depend on the country you are targeting and can be very different. In developing countries, South America and some Asian countries, or the Middle East the cost per click may be as low as two cents per click. Europe will vary between ten going to fifty cents. Scandinavian countries are relatively expensive. Same for the United

States, United Kingdom, and Australia, where clicks may be between $0.50 and over $1. You will have to set up your funnel and see what you can afford. Remember the better you can monetize your prospects, afterwards the more you can spend on advertising and outspend the competition.

There are some critics that argue that Facebook ads might be manipulated. This might be true if your objectives are likes, but I know as a fact that if you do it properly—targeting the right people and sending them out of Facebook—this is a brilliant tool. What is disputable is whether Facebook is the best media channel for all businesses. It is true that it works best in the context of entertainment, leisure, hobbies, sports, health, wealth, relationships, and fashion. Things people talk and read about in their free time. Remember we target them when they are relaxed and hanging out! If you are in the B2B space, it may be less useful, but there are ways to bridge the gap.

YouTube is the second social media I'd focus on. With over 1 billion unique monthly visitors[29] and 100 hours of video being uploaded every minute it makes it an ideal channel for any online marketer. YouTube's advertising method is called TrueView and can be accessed via your AdWords account. The strategy I recommend with YouTube is to target keywords or top videos and limit the niche with parameters like location. You can compare it to AdWords, but people are in a "semi" searching mode.

The last social media target is LinkedIn. LinkedIn is mainly used as gigantic platform to host CVs and a marketplace for job seekers and potential hires. LinkedIn is a little different from Facebook as the content is less entertainment and more business-related. People spend a lot less time on LinkedIn and don't read it like they read Facebook. It's however a huge opportunity for HR-related businesses. You can also simulate an ad and see how many people there are in your niche. LinkedIn has more than 300 million users[30], the clicks are much more expensive than Facebook, but it can be effective. Just test it out and see if it works for your business.

---

29   http://www.youtube.com/yt/press/statistics.html

30   http://press.linkedin.com/about

Of course there are many other social media we are not mentioning here, but these examples give you an idea of what can be accomplished by leveraging them.

Blogs

The next channel where we can create traffic for our site by interrupting people are "niche sites" or blogs. The business model for these sites is providing content to attract traffic and monetizing the traffic through advertisers. Compare it with magazines or newspapers in the off-line world.

What we'll look for are services or product-related sites. But how do we get on those empty spaces and put our "native" ads on them?

Three ways to do this.

First, if you know some very good compatible sites you can contact them directly and most likely they'll run your ad during a certain period and charge you a fixed price, independently of the clicks or views. Typically you will also not be able to change if it is not bringing the results you want or split test to see which ad is performing best. This is not an ideal way of advertising. You might pay for very few clicks, but it is based on the off-line model of magazines, based on numbers of readers. In the online world it's based on the number of visitors. Some more sophisticated blogs might offer you a CPM—cost per mille, or cost per thousand views—if they have the tracking set up.

The second form of media buying is through an intermediate player. There are many out there, but the easiest to start with is the GDN—the Google Display Network.

Google has created a network of thousands of websites where you can place your ads. You can set this up very easily on your AdWords account. The GDN works also on a bidding mechanism. Simplified it works as follows: You bid a certain amount per click. Google takes the available ad spaces for a certain keyword, topic or interest, goes to the highest bidder first and places that ad till the daily budget is depleted. Then it goes to the next highest bidder. Here too there are many options to rotate your ads, to show them only on certain times of the day or days of the week.

More important is the targeting of your ads. This is slightly different and essential to understand. You can either target websites that match some criteria like topic or keyword, or you can target all the websites certain types of people that you target watch. I'd definitely not recommend the last one. Media buying can be the best way to increase your business rapidly, but be careful because you can burn money very quickly. You should bid on a pay per click basis and typically 25 percent of what you bid in AdWords. These leads are not so qualified!

Start with a low budget and learn and optimize on a daily basis. But you'll have to pay for your learning curve. The same is true for the third way of buying media, which is RTB—real-time buying. Here you are also placing your ads on the places that are not filled yet, but at a lower price. SiteScout is an ideal place to start with RTB to manage your campaign. You can start with $500 and have a good control on where your ads appear.

When you start with banners always split test various designs. If the CTR of a banner starts dropping, you might consider changing it. In Online terms this is called banner blindness, which means people will not look at your banner anymore, and then you know it's time to change the ads.

If you are starting, my advice is to try social media first and later go into the media buying when your funnel is well defined.

Apps

Apps on smartphones are mainly used for small tasks or games, so be careful with the interference. People are on the go and are not in a "relaxed" state of mind. Nevertheless if you are promoting an app, it obviously makes sense. Most of the models are based on a CPA—cost per action, and you'll only have to pay when someone downloads your app. There are plenty of advertising platforms that you can choose from and it is changing very fast. Mid 2014 I consider the main players:

- Google Admob, the biggest player on the market
- Apple's iAd, for the iOS apps
- Millennial Media,
- Flurry
- Chartboost,
- RevMob
- MoPub.
- InMobi

I suggest you analyze them in detail and choose the ones that most suit your objectives and match your target audience.

In the future, mobile will be more important in terms of advertisements. Now the largest market segment is in advertising for games. As people are increasingly using their smartphones for various purposes this medium will also be used to promote other products and services. As people are behaving differently on the move than when they sit in front of their desktop you have to really evaluate this thoroughly. Location based advertising with promotions and calls to actions have a great opportunity here.

3. Informational: Press / News Releases

The business of "newspapers" has completely changed; some even discontinued their print editions, as the Seatlle post Intelligencer or Lloyd's List, world's oldest newspaper[31]. But in fact the main impact is not this transition from off- to online. Many newspapers still charge for the more in-depth online content. The dramatic change lies in what I would call the "shelf space model". In the past a printed version of a newspaper had a limited number of pages and much news content competing to be in the printed edition. Today there is an abundance of space and the content is limitless. This means that newspapers face

---

31   Lloyd's list was founded in 1734 and stopped their printing edition in 2013 in favor of a digital presence.

another challenge: to get as much content and not to cherry-pick anymore between a finite number of content pieces.

Of course the articles have to be "newsworthy" but newspapers are now more than ever looking for new content. So your task is to make their life easier and to provide them with as much content as possible. Don't mix up content with advertising, however. Your content should be noteworthy and educational, teasing the reader to come to your site. If they pick your content up this will be free traffic! A news articles is hot on the day of release, but it does not last forever. The free traffic you'll get from it will only last a couple of days or weeks. Therefore it is important to create press releases on a regular basis.

Make a list of the most important news sites in your geographic or topic area and find the main reporters that you'll send your content to. But there are also some companies such as vocus.com or www.prnewswire.com that will automatically send out your releases to the best online news sites.

Remember how you identified keywords and related key topics? Another way of getting coverage is to actually contact the specialized press, such as website blogs that are writing about your topic or related subjects. You will target all those specialized sites that are targeting your niche. And, you can give them information about your topic. You don't even have to write it yourself. Find some influential blogger, someone with a lot of followers and ask them to write you an article. You pay him, but let him also refer to the article on his blog with a link to your site! This will multiply your traffic!

4. Direct contact

A classic way to contact people is directly through a letter in the off-line world and through e-mail in the online world. You buy or rent a list of e-mail addresses and send them your e-mail. You can get qualified list from various companies such as www.infousa.com for B2C or in the B2B www.dnb.com. For B2B, another way is to create a database of people through scraping the e-mails of contacts on your prospect's websites. You might for instance want to target all architects or plumbers in your local area. You could look at the yellow page or some directory sites and collect all names ad e-mails of your target group. This is all very easy but be aware that the results might not be very good, and it can be dangerous, too! Let me explain. This way of contacting is the same as cold-calling. You contact someone that does not know you and try to tease him or her on a moment that you do not know is convenient. The prospect might be reading his mail during a meeting, in a restaurant, or even in his car, and might not be in a state of mind to listen to your message. So don't be surprised if your results are not higher than a 20 to 30 percent open rate.[32] Remember that these people who you are sending e-mails to, are people who have not opted in to receive messages from you. You might not see this as a problem, but depending on the country there are strong rules and laws, the CAN-SPAM law in the United States, that prohibits this cold-e-mailing and consider this spamming, even if you have bought or hired the list you are mailing to. Worse is that you might be caught by Google and banned so that your URL can be cancelled. In Canada the new law even foresees severe fines for spammers. If you decide to use this approach, be very cautious. If you still want to do it, the best advice I give you is to send e-mails in small batches and to put as many contact details in your e-mail, such as your company, contact e-mail, physical address, and have an unsubscribe possibility. This might reduce the chances to be seen as a spammer.

5. Partners

In the beginning of this chapter I stressed that you should not start by building your own traffic infrastructure but rather use the existing mega channels such as Google or Facebook. But there are other channels too that are great opportunities and that you can use to leverage:

   a) JV partners

   b) Affiliates

   c) Your customers

---

32   Open rate= people that open your e-mail

a) JV partners or joint venture partners are companies or individuals that already have a list of customers that matches your niche. They might be selling complementary or even similar services or products or just targeting the same niche. So why not ask them to contact their list and help you out? They will contact their list of customers who they have a relationship with—and have opted-in on their list—and offer your product. If you sell toys for kids between three and six, why not contact an e-commerce of kids' clothes? Or if you sell courses on running your first marathon, why not contact fitness related sites. The JV will normally be paid when people buy your product or service and depending on your type of product or margin get a commission varying between 30 and 50 percent. Sometimes even over 100 percent! Yes, you might give your full revenue completely away. This might come as a surprise to you, but if you have your funnel well designed you get a new customer, who is top quality and to whom you are able upsell other products! Before you contact JV partners do your homework.

Only start with affiliates when you have done the previous steps and optimized your funnel. You don't want them to be your guinea pigs. You have to show them your conversion and sales numbers. They should be motivated to sell your product. They don't want to burn their list with some "poor" products or services that are not converting.

b) Affiliates, are the second form of partnerships. The names of JVs and affiliates are often mixed. But I consider an affiliate a sales rep who doesn't really have a list but will invest in creating traffic for you. This has been a very lucrative business for many years. Affiliates typically promote products of sites such as www.cj.com or www.clickbank.com. Here you find all kinds of products that you can sell and get a commission for.

c) Your customers. Don't forget them! They might be great partners and generate you a lot of traffic. That's why you should also consider using your customers as possible partners. Do this only when they are customers. Give them the possibility to share your message

whenever you contact them. Perhaps you can give them some
bonuses if they give you e-mail addresses of potential customers
or you might even pay them. What is it worth for you to have your
customers bring back leads? Let's say that you pay $1 for every
prospect, why not give it away to your customer? He might be your
best affiliate or partner. There are some software products that
automate this process and can be a great way to create a lot of new
prospects in a short period of time. In Infusionsoft for instance you
can easily set this up.

Search	Interrupt	Informational	Direct Contact	Indirect Contact
SEA Search Engine Advertising	**Social Media** • Facebook • Youtube • LinkedIn	**Press releases**	**E-mail**	**JV Partners**
SEO Search Engine Optimization	**Blogs**	(Blogs)		**Affiliates**
	Apps			**Your Customers**

Illustration 4.5: Overview of Types of Traffic

CHAPTER 5

Convert Your Visitors and get Their E-mail

"Some cause happiness wherever they go; others, whenever they go"

Oscar Wilde

Lead Magnets

You have got through the filters of the prospects in your niche and you've got their attention so that they clicked on your ad or link. Now they are entering your world. They are your visitors! Your visitors will "arrive" on your landing page. This can be part of a website or a stand-alone page. Your objective now is to get their e-mails. The time when people gave their e-mail away for nothing has gone. Internet users are providing their e-mail less and less, because they do not want to be spammed later. It is part of someone's privacy and they will only give it in exchange for something of real value for him or her. You're in a way buying that e-mail. Your task is to give that value—the cheese—in exchange for the e-mail. It's like dating. You can't go up to someone you have never met and say, "Can I have your phone number for a date." This come-on-strong approach normally does not work. Unless you have something to offer you'll not get it. This e-mail will be the basis of further education of the customer. As in dating you'll have to build trust before you can go to the next step. Don't neglect this. You have done your work and paid for the clicks in order to get your visitor. Don't throw that money away. You have to convert as many visitors into your funnel, or in other simpler words: Get their e-mail! The key metric here will be your conversion rate. Measured by dividing the e-mails you get (the conversion) by the total unique visitors.

So how do you do that? How do you get the highest conversion rate? Some studies have showed that in fifteen milliseconds[33] people get an impression of the webpage and decide to stay further or leave directly. It is therefore very important to have coherence with the ad that brought them to your site, both in style and in offer. The "bait" or "lead magnet" has to be there. And the visitor should not have to look for it.

Psychologically the process you have to lead your visitor through is the classic AIDA[34] concept:

- Attention

- Interest

- Decision

- Action

You have to get your visitors' attention, wake their interest and then desire to finally take action and give you their e-mail. As important as coherence with the teaser that brought them to your page, you have to have a clear page where you "lead" the visitor. The main problem of most landing pages and websites is the massive clutter. Steve Krug, in his book *Don't Make Me Think* goes in depth with what you should and should not do. Marketers typically want to put as much on the website and want to highlight as many benefits as possible. But the more you highlight the more this fades out. Leading people is offering them as few options as possible. Great restaurants don't have a ten-page menu. This is the one of the main paradoxes. The more options of choice the less people decide. The same is true for your website. What you have to do is remove

---

33   Taylor & Francis online: Behaviour & Information Technology: http://www. tandfonline.com/doi/abs/10.1080/01449290500330448#.U7bA7Y2Szko

34   The term and approach are commonly attributed to American advertising and sales pioneer, E. St. Elmo Lewis

all the visual clutter. Try to be like a sculptor, remove the unnecessary wood around the trunk to get that great sculpture. You have to remove everything that is irrelevant. Don't distract the visitor. Show him what you promised and tell him what to do to get that. In a later stage you can educate him more.

The first thing that you want from your visitor is his attention. Be careful with images and videos. They absorb most of the attention and if this is not in line with what the visitor is coming for, remove them. Don't put too much text on the page. Your website should be minimalistic. Forget navigation: You don't want your visitor to escape.

The next stage you have to bring him to is to get his interest. If you have done your work properly in the ABC foundation phase you have already identified the best bait for your niche. That is also the reason why your visitor clicked on the ad and arrived on your landing page. So your task is to keep his interest and increase the desire to get it (action). Is your bait clearly placed on your site? If your visitor cannot find something easily it does not exist. Lead him to the bait. And present it in the most desirable way that they decide they want it. In a face-to-face conversation you have body language that you can identify and adapt to increase trust and credibility. The visitor should clearly see what they would get and feel safe to give their e-mail. They want to be in control. Finally tell them clearly what they have to do to get that "lead magnet." Give instructions as if you were talking to a child, taking your visitor by the hand. Don't surprise the visitor. Don't show your whiskers! Bear in mind that this is the real first impression of you that your prospect will have and as the saying goes: "You don't have a second chance to make a first impression." Consider this webpage as the book cover or trailer of a movie. Consider using some testimonials or well-known brands that have used your product or services to borrow extra trust. Also add a privacy policy, in which you state how you will handle the data of your prospects. This is often forgotten but very important.

At this point you might have various opinions on what has to be left out or included on the site, which photo to use, for example. If you follow the steps, you'll have various options and deciding which one to choose might be very subjective. At this point, in many companies it is the HIPPO, the highest-paid person's opinion, who will decide this. But this is wrong. What you should do is create the webpage and test various versions and optimize the best one. To be able to test your pages place don't forget to place analytics tools on them. Use Google Analytics to view for example the sources where your traffic is coming from, the time they stay on a certain page, the actions they take and who they are. A key metric you should look at is the bounce rate: This is the percentage of visitors who leave your page directly, without taking action or going to another page. In Google Analytics you can also analyze segments and how they behave. For example you can take all visitors coming from a certain source, the new visitors, the visitors that remain longer than a certain amount of seconds.

To help you with a better design you can use tools as www.clicktale. com or visual web optimizer (vmo. com) With these tools you can view the *mouseovers* and clicks of your visitors or simulate it. Apparently there is 80 percent correlation of eye movement and mouseover. Therefore this analysis gives you a good basis for how to improve your webpages.

But even if you have optimized your fantastic landing page the reality is that not all your visitors will convert and give their e-mail. Conversion rates are generally between 1 and 2 percent for pages doing "cold-selling". Compare this with the 3 to 5 percent in the old-time direct mail rates. It might be between 10 and 30 percent if you are offering something for free. But even if you have a fantastic offer and landing page it's rarely over 50 percent. Your visitor might be interested, but when he visited your site he was distracted or not ready yet to consume your lead magnet. So will you leave all these potential future customers and never contact them again?

No, you shouldn't. And there is a great technique to do this. It's called *retargeting*. Retargeting is a second chance to get back in front of those visitors who did not convert. So even if they did not opt in, even if you don't have their e-mail you can get back in touch. Retargeting works as follows: You place a simple script, called a tag, on your page, and when someone visits your page it places an anonymous cookie on the visitor's browser. When that person visits informational sites (news or blogs) that allow advertising or Facebook you can get in front of them via banners or text ads and tease them back into your funnel. Retargeting will only work if you have minimal traffic to your site, due to privacy reasons.[35] Most providers of retargeting require a minimum of five hundred or a thousand visits before you can start. And more important, you have to have your full funnel in place before you spend money on retargeting. With retargeting you can now show your ads only to people who already showed some interest. You can do this during a period of 30 to 90 days. However be careful with it so as not to stalk people with your ads. Therefore you can set some limits on the frequency they might see it and stop when they finally convert. Also do not forget to inform your visitors that you are applying retargeting. You can do this by mentioning it in your privacy policy on your webpage.

The most common retargeting platforms are:

- Google

- AdRoll

- Perfect Audience

- SiteScout

Each of them has advantages and disadvantages. I've summarized the most important features in the table below[36].

	Google	AdRoll	Perfect Audience	SiteScout
Bidding method	CPC	CPM	CPM	CPM
Min budget	No	$25	$25	$500
Facebook retargeting	No	Yes	Yes	No
Video retargeting	Yes	No	No	No

I would recommend to start with Google as it is the easiest and most flexible, and you will not burn your money, as could be the case with CPM, where you could potentially have no clicks. Ideally you should

---

35   You could potentially just send one identified prospect to a landing page and follow him afterwards. That is the reason why a minimum visitors is required before they allow you to apply retargeting.

36   CPC : Possibility to pay on a Cost Per Click base
      CPM: only based on a Cost Per Mil, number of impressions based

also create different landing pages or offers if you see that your returning visitors do not convert. They did not take action twice!

Retargeting can also be used to get in front of your existing customers and do some upsell, cross-sell, or down-sell. This is when you have specific landing pages for your customers, as for example upsell pages after they purchased from you. We'll cover this in the section in chapter 9, maximizing sales.

In this conversion phase the objective was to trade great information or value in order to get an e-mail. Now that you have that e-mail you will need to do something with it. In some cases we might do an immediate offer. Certainly if what we offer is a low value item. In most cases however we will need to build trust and nurture the customer before we even start pitching something. How we do that is the "cheese" for the next chapter!

CHAPTER 6

Education: Lead Nurturing

*"We are what we repeatedly do,
Excellence, then, is not an act, but a habit"*

Aristotle

Probability that a prospect will buy		
	NOW	**LATER**
Will Buy	5%	65%
Will NOT Buy	30%	

Illustration 6.1. Probability of buying now

All prospects are not equal

As a marketer you will now have the big temptation of "using" this freshly captured e-mail and send him an e-mail pitching one of your products or passing it to your sales channel. This could be a possibility if your product or service is solving some urgent need such as an express transport, a locksmith, or maybe a plumber. These might have arrived at your site via specific search terms. Even when you think they are ready you might want to "warm up" your lead. When I worked for corporate companies, I also made the big mistake of getting leads and handing them directly over to the sales teams and wondering why they were complaining about the bad quality. I had not figured out the concept of "lead readiness." Other marketers might speak about lead scoring. Today it is one of the fundamentals of the online Marketing strategy that I implement with my customers. It saves sales cost and improves their efficiency and effectiveness. To really understand this concept, we can place the leads on a graph on two parameters.

- Whether they will buy

- When they will buy

For simplicity let's only take two choices: They'll buy or not, and they buy now or they buy in the future. The numbers I've placed are made up, but the reality is often that only a very small amount will buy and is ready to do it now. However you have a very large amount that will eventually buy in the future but are just not ready now and need some time. It might be that they have to inform themselves more, evaluate choices, or find that the need is not there at the moment.

Studies have shown that 50 percent of the people that showed interest in a product but did not buy sixty days after showing interest did eventually buy it. You have to acknowledge this and build your marketing activities around it. Your role is to educate them and prepare them to decide to choose your product or service when they will be ready to buy. You have to create trust and show your expertise. The golden rule is never to pitch before you feel that the prospect is ready to buy. We would love to know when our prospect is in this ready-to-buy mode, and this is our task now to find this out. When you set up your funnel properly and start to get data of the full funnel, you will be able to fill in this table for your products or services, and then you can perfectly forecast how long you'll have to nurture your leads before they will become customers. This is really turning the slot machine into a vending machine! What will also happen in the process is that you will also "disqualify" some prospects. If in the end you'll hand over the hot leads to your sales people, make sure you also take this into consideration. The 30 percent of the lower left quadrant will never buy. They might be "interested" in your product, but not have the money or the "authority" to buy, mainly in a B2B environment. So why should you waste very expensive sales time with them?

There is a concept often used in lead qualifying and lead scoring that is called BANT. This is an acronym which *B* stands for Budget, *A* for Authority to purchase, *N* for Need, and *T* for Timeframe. *B* will be difficult to have an impact on, unless you are willing to drop your prices dramatically. But as a Ferrari dealer, would you drop your prices 90 percent so that most of the interested people "are able" to buy from you? Interest is not a synonym of the ability to buy. There is a fine line between what someone is prepared to pay for something he's interested in and what he actually will pay. Your role will be to increase his desire.

The *Authority* level is something you have to identify as quickly as possible. If someone is not "authorized" you should ask that person to pass the information to the "authority."

The remaining parameters, Need and Timeframe, are the ones that you can have a impact on through education. Your prospect might not be "really" interested or interested enough in order to buy from you? There is no connection, no trust. Building trust takes time.

The emotional bank account

In the best-selling book *The 7 Habits of Highly Effective People,* the late Stephen Covey teaches the concept of "the emotional bank account." The concept is simple: The relationships you have with other people can be seen as a bank account, in which you can deposit money or withdraw money. Every positive interaction, adding value, being kind is like a deposit to the account. Every negative interaction or—*pitching*—can be seen as a withdrawal from the bank account. These deposits are the trust you build in your prospect's mind. The more deposits you make the easier it is to withdraw money, the easier it will be to pitch. Without a certain trust level, or money in the bank account, you cannot pitch, or withdraw money!

The graph above reflects what the education process should do to your prospect's mind. Every positive interaction over time will grow the trust or goodwill. Every pitch lowers it. At a certain point you can really pitch without jeopardizing the trust you have built! As you see the more value you have provided, the less impact negative pitching has. Marketers typically are not patient enough and want the timeframe to be shortened.

The question now is: what type of content should you deliver? In the ABC foundation phase where you narrowed down the niche and identified the bait you also should have identified the different steps to achieve the desired end result that your prospect is looking for. You should now break them down in steps, like playing chess and going

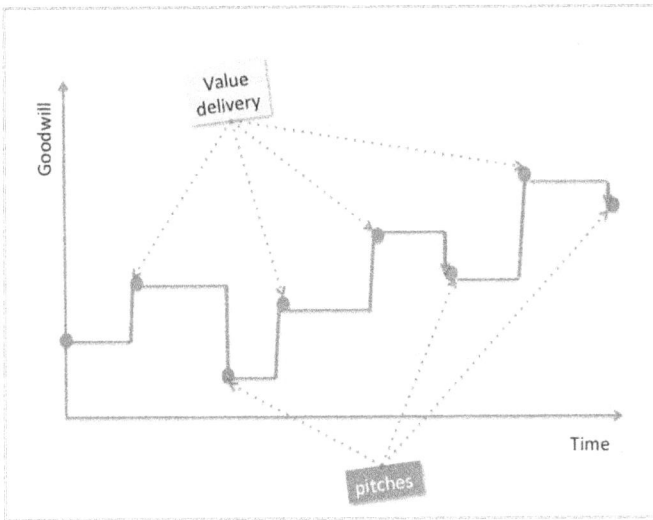

Illustration 6.2. The Emotional Bank Account.

backward from the last move to checkmate. What are the obstacles your prospects have to overcome? What is the information they need? Educate your prospect how to overcome the obstacles and solve his problems. Make a plan. The sequence is crucial. You have to make a calendar and based on the "educational" stages your prospect is in, you give him the appropriate content. Each prospect has another agenda so the content that you deliver should be individualized. This can easily be done if you automate the process.

Anticipate the top needs that your prospect will have and find out how you can make it easy for them to take the next step. Every prospect will receive the educational value pieces in a sequence and at a pace that they choose! Here you can use the power of technology and the available tools.

Every time you send something to the customer you should consider that trust building has three main parts that are:

- Create-ivity: the "value pieces" you create for the prospect

- Relationship: the act of giving free content and building reciprocity

- Leadership: helping your prospects head in the right direction

If you are providing good content that moves the prospect closer to his desired end goal that is what will create trust and eventually will create your brand within the prospect's mind, not shouting how great your product is! Consistent contact will increase the trust factor. More contacts increase "liking." The magic thing about trust is that if you have built enough trust you can even sell products that are not exactly in your field. Who you do usually ask for advice: real pitching experts or your friends?

The tools

If you have content and the e-mail of your prospect, you are good to go. The easiest and best way to educate your prospects is indeed to send them e-mails in a sequenced way.

We might make the mistake thinking that we can use and abuse e-mail because it's free.

E-mail is indeed free if you look at it technically, but sending people unsolicited or too frequent mails might not be depositing value in the emotional bank account, but rather be perceived as withdrawals and might create rejection. It is therefore important to segment your prospect list based on some triggers and adapt your e-mail frequency per segment. You can create segments based on the click activities, you can ask your prospects if they want more or fewer e-mails from you. You can ask where they are in the process of getting to their end results. You can also ask what they want to know. Your communication should be split into segments. Remember that the more "niche" we can go the better. Wouldn't it be ideal to have one-on-one e-mail? That is indeed the ultimate goal, but if you want to scale your business this will be unsustainable. That is why you need marketing automation. Great tools that you can use for this are Infusionsoft, Hubspot and Marketo. These tools allow you to build e-mail sequences based on triggers or what is most commonly named 'tags'. Tags can be anything like opening a certain e-mail clicking on a link, attending an event, filling in a survey, buying a product, or simply answering a question.

Will these e-mails reach all your prospects? If half of your prospects open your mail you are lucky or have done an excellent job. The hard reality is that you should expect that less than 50 percent will read your e-mail due to technical factors such as the deliverability factor and psychological factors: e-mail overwhelm.

Often people fill in fake addresses fearing the spam follow up. But even if you have the right e-mail address, some of your mail will not be delivered due to the deliverability score of your mailing and end in the junk folder. Every e-mail is linked to an IP address, the "@yourdomain. com." You can get your IP address from **whatismyipaddress.com**. This IP address has a "reputation" score that is created based on criteria like the bounces[37], un-subscription rates, the frequency you send mailings, number of mailings. The better the score the higher your chances of arriving in the inbox of your prospects. Do you get a lot of complaints when sending out e-mails? Do you end up with a lot of people that get to your page and quickly link away—a high bounce rate. E-mails also don't reach their destination, because the address is no longer good. How many e-mails do you send out that are returned? You can actually see your reputation at senderscore.org. The very bad IP addresses get even blacklisted and always arrive in the junk. These can be found on senderbase.org. You can improve your score by cleaning your database: Remove the inactive and bounce e-mails from your list. If possible ask for double opt-ins when asking for their e-mail so the probability of getting in to spam is lower. With a double opt-in your subscribers will receive an e-mail after they have given their e-mail or filled in a web form and have to confirm that they really want to be on your list.

Another more technical thing you can do to increase the open rate is to choose the best days of the week and hours of the day to send your mailings out. Typically mid-weekdays are great: from Tuesday to Thursday. The best time of the day you send out your e-mail is usually the beginning of the day or right after lunch. However these are averages, you have to test what works best for you because every audience is different. Don't forget to segment by geographic location

---

37   A bounce is an automated electronic mail message from a mail system informing the sender of another message about a delivery problem. The original message is said to have bounced and not delivered

and think also mobile! More and more people are reading their e-mails on mobile and this trend will increase in the future. Make your e-mails mobile friendly! When you design a website you have the advantage of custom tailoring your content for mobile and for desktop, however with e-mails you don't know how your prospect will read your e-mail. Therefore it should be readable regardless of the device. If you make html e-mails I'd recommend following some tips:

- Use body text no lower than 13px

- Use only one column

- Don't use images. Most Android devices will turn it off.

You really should do these technical improvements, however they are only the starting point, the biggest leap to make your way through the clutter of distraction and get the reader's attention is psychological. In fact we face the same challenge as we did in getting traffic: Get people to read our mail out of the maybe hundreds they receive each day. What are the keys to success? Personally I think that the two elements that will increase your e-mail open rate are to build intrigue and anticipation into your e-mails and speak one to one!

The subject line is the most important piece of your e-mail. People will decide to open—or not—the mail based on that subject line. Is the subject intriguing? Raising questions? Here are some examples that have proven to work in many industries and get high open rates:

- Top 10 . . .

- 7 Secrets of . . .

- How to . . .

- Quickly and Easily . . .

- . . . in 24 hours

- . . . Step by Step

Branding it or having a corporate style is guaranteeing a low-open rate because these elements will activate your prospects "human spam filters." Instead place a question that relates to the desired outcome. Have a pattern interrupt, confuse your prospect or just put their name as the subject. I've struggled in the corporate world to have this understood. People are so tied to the neat corporate styles. It is similar to the off-line world when you open your mailbox you sort the letters in two piles: the branded ones and the ones that you'll read.

If you have a great subject line, do follow up on that in your body copy, do not make the big mistake of not aligning the body of your mail with the subject. Your prospect will feel cheated. If you asked a question, answer it, and elaborate. Do not use the fancy templates of your mail provider; they will trigger the "spam" filter of your prospects. They might look pretty nice, but do you send your friends e-mails with a template? Perhaps you'll do that on their birthday, but not in conversational e-mails. Even worse is to brand your e-mails. These are again the biggest mistakes in design that most big companies make. Simply send a plain e-mail with white background. The language should be conversational, no ego-tripping. Your prospects want e-mails with good value helping them. A good format is plain text including a picture with a play button, as if it were a video, and linking it to the main article, a video or whatever you want to give on a webpage. Make sure that your prospects consume the content. Do not overwhelm them. Cut your content in small easy consumable pieces. It's like the bait, if they don't consume your content you might lose them in the next steps. Include anticipation in every piece. Prepare your prospects for the next mail. A great way to do this is the Andre Chaperon system SOS building your e-mail sequences like a Soap Opera Series. The success of the soap operas series lies in the open endings. Unless it is the last episode, all the series have an open end: creating anticipation, leaving a question in your mind. Our mind is very bad at coping with this. We want to close the loop; we want to know what happens next. It's like an unfinished music tune. Try this out: stop one of your favorite songs in the middle, you'll keep it in your head and hum it during a couple of hours. The same can be done with e-mails. Create a flow of stories with open endings. Leave your reader with some questions and anticipate you'll answer them in the next e-mail. Your open rates will dramatically increase. Try not to have too big intervals between your e-mails, definitely not in the beginning when your prospects are the most excited about what you have to offer.

E-mail will be your best channel to do this educational process, but I'd recommend not relying only on e-mail. Another way you can reinforce communication with your prospect: Use social media as an educational channel. A way to do this is to upload the collected e-mails into Facebook. Facebook will try to match these mails with the mails it has and create a new "custom audience." Now you can target these customers by posting on Facebook. Remember that the more they see you and hear from you the more they'll like you.

Unfortunately there is a catch. This will not be free. These people will probably not be liking your Facebook fan page, so in order to see your post you'll have to promote and pay for this. What you should do here is try to get them into your fan base so that you can communicate with them "for free." Ask them to like your page to get more great information. You might have noticed that I only recommend asking to like the fan page at this stage. The purpose of liking your fan page should only be to get a "cheaper" education, not to acquire prospects. The main purpose of using Facebook is to get people out of Facebook to your page in order to get their e-mail. Now that you have the e-mails, the objective is to nurture them and Facebook can be a cheaper way to do it. Even if you have them liking your page you will not be able to reach all of your fans for free. Facebook cleverly changed the rules some years ago and the amount of fans on which your post will appear in their News Feed will be between 6 percent and 15 percent. This will depend on the News Feed algorithm that Facebook uses. It's a kind of engagement algorithm. Facebook looks at how your fans engage with you by liking, sharing, or clicking on your posts. The more you have fans' likes the greater the likelihood that Facebook will show your post to them. It might sound strange but one of the best tactics to improve this is by regularly posting some very viral articles or videos, even if they are not related to your product or service. It will increase the engagement of your fans. In his book *Jab, Jab, Jab, Right Hook* Gary Vaynerchuk compares this technique with boxing. Post viral stuff that people will share or like and then you increase your likelihood to being seen. When you post your content the chance that it will appear in their post will be higher.

Some people like to watch videos, others prefer to read or to listen. That's why you should try to be multimodal in your education. Create a YouTube channel and start a podcast and ask them to subscribe to your channel.

Education is a broad topic and on what you "educate" your prospect will highly depend on your product or service. I have already stressed that it is important to motivate the prospects to consume your content. If you have a SaaS—software as a service, you might have been given access to a free version of your software or a free trial period. The main objective will be to help and motivate your free users to use your software. The same is true for free apps. People will not buy from you or upgrade to a paid version if they don't feel the need. A great way to motivate usage is through gamification. I briefly introduced this in the chapter on the marketing myths. The idea is to learn by playing. If you can have people use your software or app combining it with a game aspect you'll definitely have success. People love to play and share this with others in a type of competition or collaboration.

Webinars

One of the best ways to teach is live and has the full focus of your students. That's why live seminars are the best environments to educate your prospects and sell them high-ticket items afterwards. However if you have a big worldwide audience it's not always easy to do and it can be quite expensive. Excellent alternatives to live seminars are webinars or even teleseminars. You invite people for a one- to two-hour crash course on your topic, where you give them nothing else but great value. You have their attention and increase their motivation and at the end of the webinar you offer them to buy something from you. In fact webinars combine various steps of the funnel: They can be the first lead magnet, the education, and the sales offer.

Now that we have educated our prospects and set up the relationship with them, the emotional bank account should be well funded enough that we can start withdrawing some money from it –pitch. But before we start selling our core offer we can apply a technique that few marketers apply or even know. This is a concept that online marketer Perry Belcher calls the *"Tripwire."* It is meant to transform as many prospects into buyers as possible. The formula is simple: "Make a small sale before asking for your core offer." Psychologists call this the foot in the door.

CHAPTER 7

From Prospect to First-time Buyer: the foot in the door concept

"The man who removes a mountain begins by carrying away small stones"

William Faulkner

Up to now, you have identified the niches of your customers, teased them with ads, led them to your website to opt in and offered them value education. This has begun to develop your relationship with your prospects and positioned you or your brand as a credible expert in your field. Now you can motivate these individuals further to take action. You cannot rely on people buying only when they are ready. That is, you cannot say, "Let them go. When they are ready they will call us." This is what I call "hope marketing" and it is not productive. You have spent a great deal of time and effort to gain their trust. Because you have established goodwill, you are now able to contact them and ask them to take action. But, just because you have built this relationship, people will still see a relative risk in buying and making a prospect a first-time buyer is really crucial. But let's have a look at the experiences in the off-line world and try to simulate these online:

In a study conducted by Freedman and Fraser, researchers asked housewives to put a large sign advocating safe driving in their front yard. 16,7% of them accepted. In another group the researchers first asked either to sign a petition or place a small card in a window in their home or car supporting safe driving. About two weeks later, the same people were asked by a second person to put the large sign in their front yard. The results were amazing. 76% of the people who agreed to the first request now complied with the second, far more intrusive request. The very small commitment leads to the bigger one. And now that you have a trust relationship with a huge emotional bank account this step should be fairly easy. But there is even more behind this commitment.

If you are familiar with off-line retail practices, you definitely know what a *loss leader* is. It is a pricing strategy where a product is sold at a price below its market cost to stimulate sales of other more profitable goods or services. This product or service is really so cheap you feel you cannot *not buy* it. You would in fact feel bad if you didn't. This is the bait to bring in customers to your shop, to commit to a small purchase and have them buy more of the rest of what you have to offer. In buying a product there is a chemical process associated with it. You will release some dopamine[38], which modulates the brain's ability to perceive reward reinforcement. You can compare it to a certain degree as if you were taking drugs like heroin or cocaine. These will also increase the levels of the naturally occurring neurotransmitter dopamine.

After that purchase you want to repeat the experience. Haven't you had the experience of resisting eating your favorite kind of cookies, but when your willpower was weak you ate one and after that first one, you did not stop but finished the complete box. It's the same effect of that glucose drip: you want to buy more. You might be shopping for a couple of hours without buying anything, but after you bought the first thing, many other purchases followed quickly. The key was opening the wallet for the first time! This is a big difference from giving away something like you did during the conversion phase. Here there is a "shoppers' hype" taking place. And by selling instead of giving something for free you also take away the suspicion that there might be a catch. A trial or free product or service does raise some questions. You look for the fine print.

Can we replicate this process online? Yes, you can and it's even easier because you can do the selling of your core offer immediately after their first purchase. You propose to your prospects an irresistible offer, something they cannot resist to buy on impulse. The price range should be from $5 to $20, you can ask more if the perceived value is really great. It is important that there is a big difference between the perceived value and the price they'll pay. Ideally this item should be linked to what you sell afterwards. The service or product should have a good intrinsic value but should be "part of something bigger." This will motivate the purchase of that bigger ticket item. Remember the days when National Geographic sold beautiful books for nearly nothing, but ... they were part of a collection and once you bought the first or second item you felt the drive to purchase the rest of the collection. Online you could sell a software piece and sell a course afterwards or do it the other way around and sell a webinar and the software afterwards. In the past a

---

38   David Zald, associate professor of psychology, and Joshua Buckholtz, a
     Ph.D. candidate, learned that people who act impulsively—perhaps buying
     everything they see advertised on television—may have higher-than-normal
     levels of a chemical called dopamine in their brain.

lot of companies have tried to make money upselling added values. You can try to invert this process and sell these added values ridiculously cheap. In fact you could even sell at cost or even at a loss. If you have a product that is priced substantially lower than what a competitor is charging you should definitely see a big conversion.

But it is crucial to analyze your whole sales funnel and consider this step as part of the acquisition process. If you know how to make money afterwards you can put more money into the first phases: buying traffic, the bait, and the loss leader, so that you really can outspend your competitors. The real purpose is to convert as many qualified prospects into buyers.

The greater the lifetime value of the customer the more you can afford to spend on each one.

In chapter 10 from Customer to Client I will discuss how we can maximize the return on these newly acquired FTBs (first-time buyers) and how you can get this customer to come back.

Note that the shopping hype effect will be the strongest right after purchasing the loss leader, and the faster you do your upselling, the more successful you'll be. The effect will indeed decrease with time, so that even after one month the conversions compared to that from non-buyers will be a lot higher.

CHAPTER 8

From First Time Buyer to Customer: The Core Offer

"The only thing you got in this world is what you can sell.
And the funny thing is, you're a salesman, and you don't know that"

Arthur Miller, Death of a Salesman

Now that your prospect has opened his wallet and is a fresh "first-time buyer," it's time to really bring him over the line and convert him or her into a CUSTOMER. You have to motivate him for the bigger purchase. On purpose I did not consider the former step a conversion to a customer because a customer should be someone (or some company if you are in B2B) that you make a certain profit on or at least break even. In the FTB step you are still investing in the acquisition of the customer and in most cases will not yet be making a profit, definitely not if you include your traffic cost and the lead magnet. Ideally this step should come as quickly as possible after the former step. In ideal situations it should really be the next screen your prospect sees.

This step is really where the rubber meets the road. Most marketers will have this step as the second step in their funnel, if you can then speak of a funnel. This then is cold-selling. They will directly try to sell to the freshly gathered prospects without any nurturing. There might be a small part of these prospect that are ready to buy, but if you introduce the nurturing and the foot in the door principle your chances will be a lot higher in converting these prospects into customers and clients.

What we have done is nurturing the lead, we have awakened his desire to really want our product. At this point the prospect is really so "hot" that this step should be fairly easy. This is just the "closing" phase. We have placed so much goodwill and value in the emotional bank account that pitching now should not be considered as withdrawing goodwill, but a logical step in the process. In this step you will try to optimize your total revenue, not the total conversion. You have to position your price in the most optimal way: 1,000 conversions at $10 is a lot worse than 300 at $50! Therefore you should test out and see where you can position yourself.

But be careful the most important thing you should have is an irresistible offer. Your prospect should really feel bad not buying it. You brought him so far that he has the desire and now you offer him something great. You might think that getting your prospect to buy is inevitable if you have an irresistible offer. But in most cases people really need to be brought to a state of desire and be pushed a little bit. This is the case for most things in life. Here is an analogy. Let's say Susan goes over to a work associate's house. The associate says, "The kitchen is down the hall. Just help yourself to something to eat or drink." Most people will be too shy to do this unless they know the person well. They will not get any food on their own. However, if the associate brings the dish of food over to Susan and says, "Do you want some," the probability is much higher that she will take some. That's why it's important to motivate people to buy.

This is the key objective in this process: MOTIVATE to BUY. But how do we do this?

In the old school of marketing this was the role of direct-marketing pieces or the role of the salesman. That's why many copywriters have this great definition that copywriting is salesmanship in print or multiplied-salesmanship. The sales copy is meant to be the substitute for the sales rep and scale your sales.

So you should not write prose or literature. In fact the worst thing to do would be to hire a "good writer" for this phase. The key to successful copywriting is following a psychological SEQUENCE. The same as we do in our sales funnel. The words are way less important than having the right sequence.

This is not a copywriting course, but I want to give you a solid base and summarize some teachings from the big masters to ensure that your copy will work. However I strongly recommend that you read some of the best books on copywriting like *Breakthrough Advertising* by Eugene Schwartz, *Scientific Advertising* by Claude Hopkins, or take some of the courses of the late Gary Halbert[39], Gary Bencivenga[40], John Carlton[41], or Perry Belcher[42].

The right sequence:

You can split the content in many parts. Perry Belcher has a great 21-step formula for a sales letter, but I prefer to bring it into a seven-step formula:

---

39   http://www.thegaryhalbertletter.com/

40   http://www.marketingbullets.com/index.htm

41   http://www.marketingrebel.com

42   http://www.usonlinedigitals.com/product/perry-belcher-ryan-deiss-secret-selling-system

1. Grab the attention with a HEADLINE and sub-headline

2. Describe and expand their—Urgent—PROBLEM

3. Give them a—UNIQUE—PROMISE or SOLUTION

4. Substantiate this with PROOF that your solution will work

5. Make an irresistible easy and user-friendly PROPOSAL

6. Call to ACTION

7. Recap the benefits and proposal

It is crucial to follow this sequence. You cannot skip or switch the steps. Compare it with dating. There is also a sequence. You don't ask to marry someone after the first chat. Some people argue that long sales letters or long pitches do not work. This is completely wrong. Indeed, many prospects will not read your long sales letter or listen to the whole pitch, but those are the people that are not interested in what you have to tell them. People don't give you their money without giving you their time. That's why webinars or live seminars are so great to sell to people. The more time they spend with you, the more likely they will buy from you. I have personally seen an online marketer—I won't mention his name—sell a 30,000- dollar Mastermind course[43] live to an audience of 250 people where 62 people applied for it in 10 minutes. Of course it was not 10 minutes but the whole education and the 2-day seminar before that contributed to this conversion!

So let's dive a bit deeper into these seven steps.

1. Grab the attention with a HEADLINE and sub-headline

---

43   Mastermind is referred to as Napoleon Hill describes it in his book *Think and Grow Rich*. The mastermind group is designed to help you navigate through challenges using the collective intelligence of others

The first step is the one you'll also use for your e-mail. In direct mailing it used to be the key element. We have already elaborated on headlines in the educational phase. This is really key if you want to have the chance to pitch to them. So unless you offer your product or service directly after the former step without an e-mail you better choose a good one. The headline should already include a PROMISE or provoke your prospect in an intriguing way. Curiosity is great and will work, but it's even better to include some great benefit. This will mostly outperform the former. It's not easy to come up with great headlines and therefore it's good to brainstorm and make at least twenty proposals and then edit and choose the best ones to test them out! Start with a headline that you think will work, the control headline, and compare it to your new creations. One thing you should not forget is not to see the headline as a separate piece of the puzzle. It should be integrated in the rest of your pitch. You'll tease your prospects and bring them to your landing page, but if the copy or video is completely out of sync with it they'll be lost! So if your headline is working you bring them on your landing page where you restate your headline and substantiate this with the sub-headline. If you have used a promise in your headline the sub-headline should briefly explain *how* your product or service will fulfill this. Explain the mechanics. But very briefly! Don't make additional promises; just validate what you stated in the headline.

2. Describe and expand their—Urgent—PROBLEM

Once you have them on your landing page and after your headline and sub-headline intro, here you start by identifying their problem. You should speak the same vocabulary. Try to explain their problem or desire better than they can themselves.

A quick note on needs and wants. We usually mix these words but there is a big difference and we have to understand this in our marketing. A need is really to fulfill a basic necessity such as water, air, food, shelter, basic clothing, or transportation. The need for food is an important issue in some developing countries, but in developed countries most people will base their decisions on wants. They have the choice. So if we have the choice it's rather a desire or want than a need. Your goal in this step is to elaborate on the desires or problems for which the desire might be a solution. You expand on the desire or make the problem worse. You pile the desires up. Try to make the desire more urgent.

Imagine that you sell alarm systems. You might stress that in the last year the number of burglaries in the neighborhood of your prospect has increased significantly. You can support this with some figures and show the big problems that this has caused.

If you sell a language course, you might stress on the benefits that knowing an extra language involve: the better jobs, the independence,…

3. Give them a—UNIQUE—PROMISE or SOLUTION

Now you reveal to them your solution. You should not talk about the features but about the benefits. We want to think that we are rational buyers but the reality is different. Except some professional (B2B) buyers, we normally act on emotional triggers and after we have purchased something we try to rationalize our actions. A car might have the following features: 200 horsepower, 6 airbags, 30 miles per gallon. The benefits are faster driving, protection of my family, and saving money.

So we have to build on the benefits of our product or service. But don't mention too many benefits; ideally you should concentrate on one. Every benefit you mention, you should substantiate and prove afterwards. If you fail to do it for one of them, you'll lose your credibility and your pitch will be weak.

The human brain will try to find these weak points in your pitch. The best promise should be one UNIQUE benefit, the unique selling proposition or USP. The more unique the better, if the benefit is important enough to fulfill the desires of your audience. This uniqueness should contrast with former solutions or solutions of the competition. If you have done your foundation work properly you should just use it now.

An ideal way to describe this benefit is projecting your prospect in the future by saying: "Imagine . . ."

"Imagine what your life would be with this benefit, with this solution. Compare this with where you are now!"

4. Substantiate this with PROOF that your solution will work

The proof is the most important piece of your sales pitch. Proof alone can sell. It's the strongest part but also the most difficult to find. This requires work but it's what the prospect is looking for. Without proof the distrust remains. By now you should have created a lot of trust with your prospect, but he or she will still look for this extra piece of proof in order to really purchase from you. You'll have to substantiate this enough in order to convince the prospect that you or your product is the right solution for him. Some of the best ways to deliver proof are:

- **Demonstrate that something works**: If your product allows it, show a recorded video where your product is in action. This is one of the most powerful methods. Blendtec did this blending an iPhone and other items. Have a look at it. It was so powerful that it has gotten also over twelve million views: https://www.youtube.com/watch?v=qg1ckCkm8YI&gl=BE If you can do this it really blends everything!

- **Testimonials**: Social proof is very powerful and should be used as much as possible. Think of all the ratings, likes, and shares. In chapter I'll reveal how you can use your former customers to help you with it.

- **Endorsement from an authority**: If an authority can be linked to your product this is also very powerful. It's better if it's related to your niche, but even if it isn't, it can work. One of the authorities to use is the prospect's friends! We love to ask trusted people for advice. But with the education and great value you have given your prospect so far by now you should also be a trusted expert. If you or your product have been featured on popular media or the local newspaper you can borrow this, too.

- **Explain the mechanics of your product or service**: The proof can be found in how it is built.

- **A creative guarantee:** like a 120 percent money-back guarantee, try it free. Only pay if you get results.

- **Specialization:** If you are "the specialist of a niche" that will also give a lot of credibility. Researches have proven that specialization builds trust among Web users. In a study conducted by the Penn State University researches randomly assigned a group of students to buy wine on a website. They were helped to make their choices by recommendation agents. There were 2 groups and the conditions were identical. The only difference was that in the first group the recommendation agent was called a "wine agent" and in the second group it was identified as an "e agent". The participants trusted the "specialized" technology significantly more than the general one. Apparently this is a general rule and the more specialized layers there are, the more trust is perceived. Researches explain this as mental shortcuts that help us decide. We see this constantly in life: a statement made by someone with a white uniform is perceived as more credible, a long essay is seen as a strong essay.

- **Acknowledge disbelief:** Your main goal with your sales copy is to tackle all objections a prospect might have. But sometimes the disbelief is so strong that the best and most credible way is to acknowledge them. Admitting shortcomings of your product is very powerful. But these should not be related to the main benefits of your product. The trick here is to admit less important benefits while reinforcing the main benefits.

The proof is really crucial. If your proof is strong enough like the Blendtec example, your copy can be weak. But bear in mind not to focus on too many benefits. Every belief you have to suspend, you'll need proof for and substantiate.

5. Make an irresistibly easy and user-friendly PROPOSAL

Now you propose your OFFER. What you will exchange for the money. It's important that your prospect perceives the offer as something easy to use, user-friendly. Be very clear and explain in detail what you have to offer. Ideally here you can also add some bonuses. Bonuses do not have to strictly relate to your offer. And tell them the PRICE. It is extremely important to justify the price compared to something they know or commonly buy. Bring it back to a daily cost. Justify the price for the time and money invested, such as courses taken and more important try to juxtaposition your price: "normally it costs x, but today you'll get it for—" Try to split your service or product in value pieces and show the price of every piece. The sum of the pieces should be a lot more than the price of your offer. Some people argue that people buy on price or you might think that your product is too expensive. But look at it from a weighing-scale perspective. The price you ask should be equal or less than the sum of the desires to buy your product. So instead of lowering your price it would be better to try to increase the desires, sharpen or expand the problem, and show the benefits of your solution. This is value-based pricing!

Another aspect that you should take into account when proposing your offer is the risk perception. People fear every time they have to open their wallet. Every purchase has a risk associated to it. And I do not only mean a financial risk—losing the money in case the product is not meeting their expectations, but also they might feel "stupid" for their "irrational purchase" that they cannot rationally justify afterwards. Often the risk the customer is taking is higher for the customer than the seller. At least that will be the customer's perception. Your objective should be to lower the risk for your prospect as much as possible. For example, let's say I am going to help to build your website.

I could propose to do this for $10,000 to cover the design and development of your new site. Take it or leave it: That's it. Whether or not the design works is your problem. I'll do the work and get my money. But you do not know the end result. In this case, I am placing 100 percent of the risk on you. On the other hand, I could say, "I will do your design, and you will pay only if you get the agreed results afterwards. We'll define this for example as x leads per day." In this case I take the whole risk. This 100 percent risk approach can be quite successful for two reasons:

1. You don't have to convince your prospect by telling them all the benefits. The proof is built in!

2. People are attached to future money. We prefer to use credit cards and pay afterwards.

This approach where the seller assumes 100 percent of the risk is becoming quite common. In fact most of the app business is based on it. Download it for free and pay only when you really need it or want more. In e-commerce free shipping has also become a standard. According to comScore, free shipping is becoming the norm. Particularly around holiday time, as many as 49 percent of e-commerce businesses offer free shipping. Companies like www.zalando.com that sell shoes are even going a step further: They offer free returns. You can order some pairs, try them on, and have thirty days to return them if they don't fit—all with free shipping and returns—even though they have 30–40 percent return rates. This practice has indeed lowered the barrier of buying shoes online drastically.

Now that you have proposed your offer it's time to get your prospect to take action.

6. Call to ACTION

You should not expect that the prospect will take some action if you don't ask him. As stupid as it might seem, most missed sales are due to the lack of detailed description or being too vague about what your prospect has to do. Detail the steps: "Push on the button below, fill in your name and credit card details." You should really be talking to a kid or a dummy, but it's proven that this is the way to do it. These steps should really be like commands, not requests.

One point you cannot forget is to add some scarcity into the sales process. You can do this by means of only having the offer for the next twenty-four hours or next couple of days. A timer will really help with this. If you don't discount your product you may remove the bonuses if they do not take action. Even though we know that some of these scarcity techniques are made up we fear losing the opportunity. You might even stress this by adding: "If you don't take action now you won't have it." The fear of loss is always bigger than the desire to succeed. But

I advise you to be honest with your scarcity, otherwise it will not work in the long run!

7. Recap the benefits and proposal

The last part of the sales letter is the PS or PPS. And here you should take the opportunity to recap the whole sales pitch but in reverse mode: "What will happen if you do not take action now." The PPS can be used to recap some single benefits and motivate them to read more of the sales letter.

In fact most people read sales letter as follows: They read the headline and sub-headline, then they go and look for the price, and if they are motivated to buy go back and read either from top to bottom or in reverse order. But they mainly read in order to find some inconsistencies.

But the sales letter is not the only communication mode you will use. Online there are different modalities that you can do your pitch:

- A classic (long) sales letter

- A Video Sales Letter (VSL): This is cutting your sales letter down in pieces and animate them with a PowerPoint or keynote presentation. But only using text. As strange as it might seem, this works really well and is one of the best ways to present your offer.

- The classic video: a recorded video with more visual content than just text.

- A webinar or teleseminar: If your product or service is suited for it, this is definitely the strongest approach. You will have the attention of your prospects during an hour to an hour and a half and have the opportunity to bring them to a state where they really are eager to buy. The conversion rates are typically the highest here. In the off-line world the same happens with live seminars. Definitely if you add some scarcity or extra bonuses for the quick decision takers.

The first three modalities will be hosted on a landing page, and the most common way to bring your customers to one of these modalities is via e-mail. You can also do a direct *upsell* after the former step. For those people buying the "loss leader" product, you can bring them directly to your landing page. This should be the most effective way of taking advantage of the psychology behind the "consumer's hype."

CHAPTER 9

Maximize Sales

"If the pie is getting smaller, then reinvent the pie"

Dan Sullivan

Maximize sales

This first sales transaction should not be the end objective of your funnel, but only a beginning. Now the real monetization starts. Many businesses do not exploit this enough. If you want to increase your sales you have three options: Get more customers, get them to buy more frequently, or you try to get more sales out of the transaction. Getting new customers is the whole process I've described till this point, and you know that it is a lot more expensive to find a new customer than to sell to an existing one. Having the customer come back is indeed easier, and I'll describe this in the next chapter. But the best way to increase your business is through maximizing the current sales through upselling, cross-selling, or selling a product bundle. This has never been as easy as it now is online. Most of the up or cross-sell is pure profit, and it's crucial to understand that if you are able to improve this step, you will be able to spend a lot more in acquiring customers and beating the competition.

Upselling or cross selling has often had a bad connotation. People are being sold something extra they do not need, and I don't mean you should do this. No one wants to be "upsold" or pushed to buy more. However this practices should be a positive thing. Think about it. When you buy a suit, perhaps you want a complementary tie? When you buy a car an extended warranty could be something you value, or imagine you are leaving Disney World, wouldn't you like to buy a souvenir to remember the great moment you had with your kids?

Whatever you sell, there is always some complementary product or service you can offer your customer. And ideally this should be offered right after the main sale. Remember that you have created trust with your customer. The customer knows you and now you also have a relationship with him. So why not propose it. Your customer is still in the hype of buying and might want something extra. It's important to understand what you can sell in order to maximize your process.

There are five main types of "extra" sales that can be categorized as follows

a. Upselling

b. Complementary services or products

c. Continuity

d. Similar products

e. More of the same

a. Upselling

The first maximizing opportunity is offering some extension of the product. People might have a desired end result in mind and the product or service that you sold them will help them get that result. However they might want to have it quicker or with less hassle. With every purchase there is some small or bigger learning curve to use the product or service to its full capacity. Therefore you might offer them services that will shorten this and lead to quicker results. Here you might include services like "made for you"; a tool that will help them implement your course or a course to learn how to use your product or service more in-depth. The upsell might be filling in some missing pieces of your service or product. Typically the upsell will be at least as expensive or more than your core product.

You might even offer some consulting or coaching, but because these services are typically more expensive I'd recommend leaving your newly acquired customers a while in order that they use your product or service and after they are happy with it, have been able to use it, then ask them whether they might want some extra help. Ideally you can organize a webinar to give them extra value again—going back to the education phase—before asking them the magic words "do you want some help."

b. Complementary services or products

You might also offer your customer some added-value services. These include things like warranty extension. It might also be more or new features of your product. The best example is a car. You want to buy a car. You will be offered electronic options, Internet in the car, better audio, extra warranty, leasing options. You might think your product is not suited for that, but if you reduce some standard features you can create some added values: e.g., more bandwidth if you sell some SaaS, extra or better support, more credits or accounts. The big difference with the upsell is that the extra sales will typically be less than the core sales. Often the term "upselling" is also used for this in business, e.g., you sell a deluxe room instead of a standard room. In this example the "extra sales" is the difference between the standard room and the deluxe room. Unless you are lucky to sell a presidential suite, the difference is less than the core value (the value of the standard room). I prefer to make a distinction between both. It is the tie when you sell the suit! The reason is that you can try to upsell your bigger ticket item and if your customer does not buy this, offer these complementary services, which in relation to their purchase might have more success.

A strategy that you might apply here is bundling your core offer with some of these complementary services. For the upsell you can also include them as bonuses. This is a great strategy to increase the value perception, definitely if you are competing with a more commoditized product.

c. Continuity

This might be one of the most lucrative in the long-term. This might be access to a premium subscription or a closed forum to get more out of your purchase. The power here is that you are selling continuous education. They will now pay you to educate them further and you get a continuous revenue flow for this!

d. Similar products

"Customers who bought this also bought that." You know this from Amazon.com. This is typically a "cross-sell." You offer a product that is not directly linked to your core sale but that is in the sale "market." Typically you should have similar prices not higher. The idea behind these extra sales is that you are leveraging the "buyer's hype," as you did with the "loss leader" in the step converting from the first-time buyer to customer. You should however offer services or products that are relevant to your market and to your niche. Amazon discovered this a decade ago, and today more than 60 percent of their sales are coming from this process. If you bought or are buying a book on educating your Labrador, why not buy another one on how to better feed your dog?

e. More of the same

Some products can be sold in quantities, so why not offer this also online. You might not sell two courses to the same person but what about selling "packs" of three body lotions or five pairs of socks. Nearly all consumables can be sold in multiples. Even items that you would not think of as books are good candidates. Just propose to buy two or three of the same book to offer to friends. You can also be more creative and offer to buy some items in advance at a lower per item rate but only deliver them when they need it. Audible.com, a subsidiary of Amazon does a great job on that. You prepay on a yearly basis and every month you get a new credit that you can use to download an audiobook. What you have to do here is put the multiple prices in perspective to the individual price, e.g., they just bought one lotion at $30. If you buy two more you get them for \$15 each. You can really decrease your price a lot because you do not have to include your acquisition cost, so every bit on top of the marginal cost of each extra item is pure bottom-line profit!

These are the main possibilities you can offer your customers. Once you have decided what to offer you need to design a flow of how and when to offer this

It is crucial to incorporate this phase automatically in your sales funnel and based on some actions offer different options. You might even include an upsell in different payments if they do not buy directly. The power here is that you can really personalize your actions. Every customer can be sold differently based on their actions. This was really tricky to do before in the off-line world, even online. Today however customer relationship management software tools like Infusionsoft, Marketo or even Aweber make this very easy. Look at a simple but effective example below that you can easily implement and upsell after a customer purchases something.

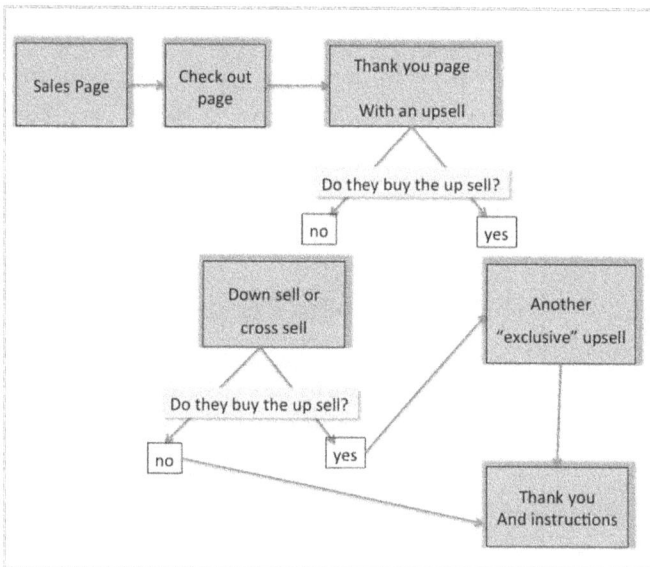

Illustration 9.1.: Example of a Flow to Maximize your Sales.

CHAPTER 10

From Customer to Client: Leverage your Return On Relationship

"The purpose of business is to create and keep a customer"

Peter F. Drucker

I've been many times to Venice in Italy and I find it one of the most magical places on earth. However I'm often frustrated about the quality of the service and the food at many of the restaurants there. And I can assure you I love Italian food. The reason for these bad experiences is that they see the customer as a one-time transaction and believe that 90 percent or more of these visitors will not come back. So why bother to give these tourists a WOW effect or decent experience. The quicker they can get rid of the customer the quicker they can place a new one at a table. This practice might have worked in the past but in this new era with all the social media review sites there is a greater transparency and in the end they will suffer. The good will be better and the bad will be worse. To illustrate this, look at the example in TripAdvisor.

Don't fall into the trap of the typical tourist restaurant where the end goal is only to make more transactions. You don't want to see them only as a once-in-a-lifetime customer rather than using the transaction as the beginning of a lifelong relationship. Leverage the great opportunity that social media offers! You should consider the *Life Time Value* of each customer: What is the expected value that an average customer will spend till he stops using your services or products or till he switches to the competition. We can evaluate the previous steps of the funnel, in

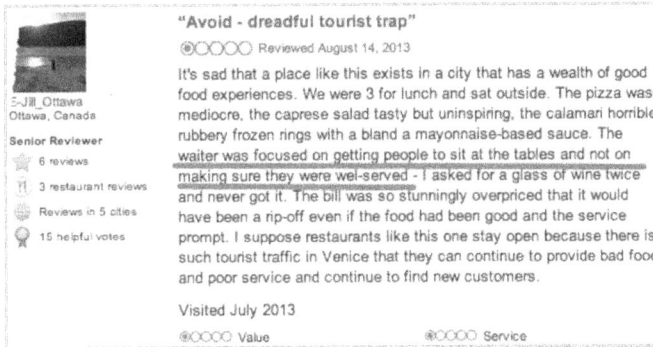

"Avoid - dreadful tourist trap"

◉○○○○ Reviewed August 14, 2013

It's sad that a place like this exists in a city that has a wealth of good food experiences. We were 3 for lunch and sat outside. The pizza was mediocre, the caprese salad tasty but uninspiring, the calamari horrible rubbery frozen rings with a bland a mayonnaise-based sauce. The waiter was focused on getting people to sit at the tables and not on making sure they were wel-served - I asked for a glass of wine twice and never got it. The bill was so stunningly overpriced that it would have been a rip-off even if the food had been good and the service prompt. I suppose restaurants like this one stay open because there is such tourist traffic in Venice that they can continue to provide bad food and poor service and continue to find new customers.

Visited July 2013

◉○○○○ Value   ◉○○○○ Service

Illustration 10.1: A TripAdvisor review of a restaurant

which we created our customer as the cost and effort, but now we enter in a return on relationship (ROR). This process should be a lot easier and will get better results but in many cases a lot of companies do not take the time to invest in it. You might have heard many times that it is easier to sell to existing customers than it is to acquire new ones. Today this statement is even more relevant for various reasons:

1) The customer knows you well. If you have done proper work in your funnel, the new customer already knows you, he trusts you; you have had your first relationship with him. You are not a foreigner to him, but he should see you as the "expert." He bought from you. This is indeed a big step. If he likes your services or product—and you should always try to deliver the best you can—it should be easy to have his attention for further communication. You shouldn't spend a lot to get through the noise, and you don't have to do all the initial nurturing.

2) You know the customer. You should have more information about him. At least you have some interaction and transactional data. What did he buy, what did he download, or click on. How long did the process last? Perhaps you have asked some pertinent questions along the way in order to be able to segment

him better and try to have a one-on-one communication with him.

Your task now is to maintain the relationship and improve it even further.

The first thing you should do right after the first transaction is to create a WOW effect. It's true that in today's world it is increasingly more difficult to surprise people and give them experiences beyond their expectations. We are used to instant gratification. Next-day delivery is not enough anymore. We don't have patience. We are easily distracted. We have all the info at our fingertips. Even going on a trip where you haven't been before is not a big novelty anymore. We look at Google Earth, see some videos only or have a virtual tour of the hotel where we are going to stay. So how can we create a WOW effect in this environment? You could even argue that the expectations of our customers are so high that when we deliver our product or service it can create a negative effect because our customer expected more. But there is good news . . .

In business environments there is still a huge opportunity because most companies stop the sales process right after the transaction. They've received the money so let's go hunting for a new customer. You see it over and over again. I'm always amazed that when you buy a car, even very expensive cars, and you have to wait months—sometimes as long as nine months—to have your car delivered, you don't hear or see anything till the car is there. No e-mail, no communication at all!

Don't speak about a WOW effect. The day of delivery you might receive a call that you can come and pick up your car. What a waste of opportunity. People really desire their new car, like a kid waiting for his Christmas presents. Why not communicate how the process goes, or what you can do with your new car. Give some pre-education. Show some testimonials . . . This is so easy and your customers will talk about it. They will share your message with their friends and relatives.

But there is more than this of course. The relationship with your client has various objectives:

1. Extend this in time as long as possible. Have the customer RETURN to you as often as possible

2. Make him or her an indirect promoter of your business through RATING and COMMENTING on his experience

3. Find the ambassadors that will be direct promoters of your business though REFERRALS and AFFILIATION

This is the process of relationship with your clients: R^3 (Return—Rate—Refer). I'll now dig a bit deeper into each of these objectives, so that you will have a good understanding what you have to do.

#1 Return

We have acquired a new customer, so what do we have to do to transform him into a lifetime client and have him return and buy again from you? It's important that you segment your clients as well as you can. Each of them will have different needs and a different time-frame, but you can identify three phases that you should tackle differently.

- The delivery phase
- The nursing period
- The "after" period

The length will differ from product to product, but most services and products will have these cycles.

As mentioned above you have to find ways to impress your customer. Think what a customer will need or do just before, during, or after the purchase. Who will he relate with? What will he do? What might he need? And try to leverage this. That is where you can surprise him and even obtain a WOW effect. Take for example the purchase of a car, house, or even a new iPhone; something that increases someone's status. After the purchase or before delivery your client will definitely want to share it with his friends and relatives.

You can find ways to improve this *"delivery" phase*. But don't overcomplicate it. Even a simple thank-you postcard can create the desired effect. A good place to find examples is in top hotels. They have to look continuously for new ways to deliver a dream-come-true experience. If you use this in other businesses you might get incredible results. This will then be the start of a—we hope—long relationship with your CLIENT.

After impressing your client you will make sure that he uses your product or service. This is a basic requisite if you want to have a further business relation with your client. He bought it with an end goal in mind. You should now help him to achieve the end goal in the best way possible. To do this I recommend a *"nursing" phase*. Like a newborn child, your client needs help to use the product or service. Tutorials are great for this. But don't think the customer will find his way easily to your website where you posted the tutorials. You will have to e-mail him with the appropriate links. This is like the second education phase, but now more technical. Depending on your product your clients can have different end goals and a different agendas. Therefore segmenting your customer base is crucial. This is another advantage of your online strategy. You should know you customer by now; you might have asked him more detailed questions about his business or personal life. You should have recorded not only his transaction, but also all the interactions with you. Did he click on some links? Did he watch certain videos? Did he download some papers? All this information should have been tagged and should now allow you to do a proper segmentation job. Even if you have, but certainly if you haven't you can also ask more information through a survey (surveymonkey.com or fluidsurveys. com).

The extra advantage you get from surveys is that you can also adapt and improve your product with the input provided. You can have a real two-way communication. But don't limit the communication to simple e-mails. You can send also some postcards or set up a Closed Facebook Group for your clients only, where they can help each other.

Once the nursing phase is over you should stay in contact with your client on a frequent basis. It's really crucial and most businesses fail here. You know the saying: "Out of sight, out of mind." I suggest you should really plan this in advance. Identify the key phases in your product lifecycle and try to send some communication on those key moments. Also calendar the important events where you can contact your customers, like their relatives' birthdays, Christmas, Valentine's, Easter, Thanksgiving, start of school, holidays or New Year. Try to fully automate this process, so that no one will be forgotten. Often companies rely on CRM tools to place as much information as they can and have of the customer in a tool. CRM has been a big buzzword for more than two decades. Companies have really paid millions for tailor-made CRM tools. But rarely have I seen good usage of these tools, except perhaps in managing the sales force, but definitely not for improving the communication with the customer, mainly because most CRM tools know a lot about the customers' DNA, like gender, age, address, marital status in case of an individual or company size, turnover, contacts for a business, and combine this with transactional data. But very few if any information is captured of the interaction of the customer, let alone the online behavior. And it is just this behavioral data that is key to improve your communication and delivering the right message at the right time through the right channel. Focus the communication in delivering great value to increase your perception with the client. This will improve the goodwill and you'll be able to do more business with them.

You can improve the value of your clients by either having repeat purchases of the same product or offering higher-end products, like coaching or consulting. But you can also start selling related products: a line extension. You are now a trusted partner and you can start selling related products in your niche to improve the value you get out of a client.

Another way is to find ways of increasing the frequency of usage through continuity programs. This is like having a monthly or yearly fee and having limitless (or more) access to your service. Good examples are fitness centers or carwashes. You offer unlimited access for a monthly fee. People will use it more often and you are securing monthly income. Even if you don't have a service you can create a monthly continuity program, create a course, or give some technical support.

#2 Rating and Commenting

When you are uncertain often you decide based on the opinions of others. Think of the last time you wanted to book a hotel, or chose a restaurant when you were visiting London or New York. You go to sites such as www.booking.com or www.tripadvisor.com and look at the ratings or comments of others. Also when you buy something, don't you look at the comments on Amazon? Even when there are no ratings or comments online, we ask our friends on Facebook, or look at some forums. We are so used to it. It's like a THEY (the seller) versus US (the buyer). And we believe "the weakest" site; the buyer's opinion.

Social proof is so important today and people love to comment, like, or share stuff online. It has become part of our life. At the end 2013 the average number of daily likes on Facebook alone was 4.5 billion! Look at the success of rating sites like www.yelp.com that get over 100 million visitors per day! It shouldn't be a surprise that the big companies use the ratings and number of comments as a key parameter for their ranking algorithms: Google for the search results, Amazon to rank the products; Facebook to show post and Apple to rank the Apps.

I cannot stress enough how important these rankings are for your online strategy. It is a lever to most of the steps in your funnel. Whether you try to attract, convert, educate, or want to sell, social proof is a key element. And now that you have a created a relationship and trust you have to leverage this! And if you can get testimonials from your clients it's even better.

So, what can you do to get this higher ranking? Enhance and motivate people to rate or comment on your product or service. You have to ask it. Build an automatic e-mail to ask for comments, how they rate your service or product and ask about their experience. Make it easy for them, but beware that people are seven to ten times more likely to leave a bad review than a positive one. The negatives will come automatically but the positives you have to stimulate. Be sure that you only ask proactively people that have used your product or service; those that really have experienced it. In an app for instance you can build this in and start asking only those people that have used your app at least five times to rate your app. The probability of them ranking your app will be higher. Asking people is also a way of keeping in touch with your customers.

Even so, your clients will give you some negative comments. These comments should allow you to improve your product. It's crucial to have a two-way conversation and answer these comments. Never blame a customer or get into a discussion even if you don't think he is right or didn't use your service or product in a proper way. Acknowledge his comment, apologize, and try to give value and do this publically!

Beware about trying to beat the system by placing false reviews. Google has penalized sites for doing this. Companies trying to play with algorithms have become a big problem. Sellers can go to a site such as www.fiverr.com and have people download their app in return for a five-star rating. With higher-priced services, such as a hotel, the person needs to have actually stayed there to write a review. But, with lower-ticket items, sellers can ask people to buy it and rate it. So, a lot of cheating goes on. Just make sure that they are the real thing. After someone makes a purchase, motivate that person to write a review.

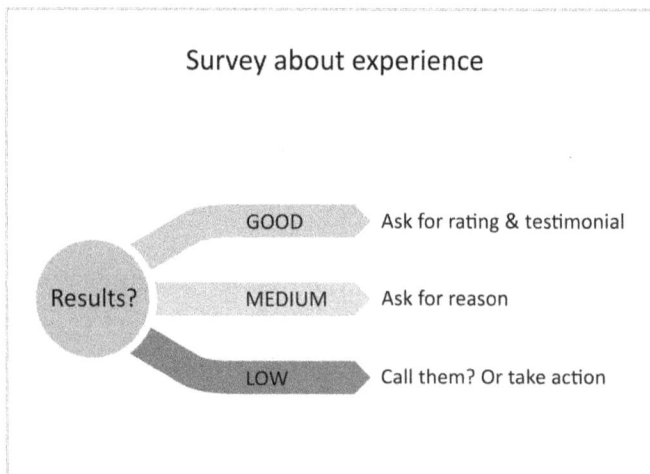

Survey about experience

Results? → GOOD → Ask for rating & testimonial

Results? → MEDIUM → Ask for reason

Results? → LOW → Call them? Or take action

#3 Refer and Affiliation

The ultimate desire for a company is that your product or service spreads virally. Unfortunately this is the case only in rare occasions. I sometimes hear that marketers want to design a strategy to make the product viral. Personally I think this is like hoping that it rains in the desert during summer. If you understand some of the basics of why some things go viral and others do not, you can increase the likelihood that you'll get some free advertising.

One of the key ingredients is social currency. To get a better understanding look at young children. What do they do after drawing a picture? They all do the same thing . . . show it to their parents. This sharing continues through our life. We want to show the car, the house, and the clothes we bought. We want to share our holidays, our achievements. They say that people that climb Mount Everest feel more happiness in sharing it afterwards in base camp than the moment they reached the top. But it's not only about purchases, experiences, but also about our opinions and what we like. This is also the main reason that social media has grown so quickly. It created the perfect platform to share even more. But we don't share everything. We prefer to share things that we like or things that may make us look good. Every "share" is like a social currency. We want to be associated with what we share. This can even lead to people who are not real experts on a topic but curate information and share the best things about it to be seen as experts. But it also means that people will normally be selective in sharing, because of this social currency. And you should therefore only motivate your clients that are really raving fans of your product. They have to feel associated.

I often get asked if it would be a good idea to do a member-get-member action (MGM). Personally I don't think it is a good idea. You cannot buy referrals. People will do it intrinsically. Not because they want to help you or be paid, but because they want to do it for themselves.

Let me give you an example. Imagine you ask me for a good restaurant in Brussels—I'm from Belgium by the way—and I give you the name of *Le Chalet de la Forêt*. Even if you go there and you liked the food, you'll love it, but afterwards hear that I'm getting paid for every person I bring to the restaurant, my credibility or social status will decrease in your eyes.

As I described in the chapter on the ABC foundation when you select a target you should get very focused and narrow down your niche. The same is true for finding the clients or partners that will bring you leads. Those are your good customers that know, trust but above all like—or love—your product or service and have a good following on social media.

Most referrals happen when we are in a conversation with someone about a topic and relate our own experience with it. Let's say you are talking about lower back pain with your friend and remember you had a great experience with a chiropractor. You directly recommend it to him. Notice that this recommendation is free (1), you don't get compensated for it, (2) you have used his services and had a great experience (3) with him. Another example is if a headhunter asks you if you know a good candidate for a certain job. Most likely you'll only pass him candidates that you have worked with or know very well and had a great experience with. You don't want to lower your "social status".

If we translate this into our business, we have to identify the clients that will recommend using two main parameters: They have to be on one hand happy clients that believe in your product and on the other hand influencers with a good network.

They have to be confident clients that believe in your product, this means that they have bought it, used it, and got their desired end result. And you should be the reference for them in for the product or service category. An effective way to segment these is through the RFM method. Remember that *R* stands for Recency, *F* stands for Frequency, and *M* stands for Monetary Value. We identify the most recent purchasers that have bought often with the highest total purchase value. In most businesses, twenty percent of the customers make up eighty percent of the business. If you dig deeper: twenty percent of those twenty percent, or four percent, make up 64% of the total business. This is true in most industries. Your task is now to nurture them and build a splendid relationship. Hence the constant communication!

Besides being a good client—and friend—you should also find out if they have a good following on social media; do they have many friends on Facebook? Are they actively posting and sharing? Do they have a blog? You should identify them. This parameter is even more important than the first. Many tools exist today that will help you identifying these influencers so that you can transform them into your marketing ambassadors.

Once you have identified your fans, the objective should be to motivate them to bring you leads. As I've said, they will not do this to do you a favor, except perhaps if they are relatives or good friends. They will do it because they want to raise their status with their friends. How do you motivate them without paying for this?

Referrals happen in a conversation about a topic.

- Your fan should notice that the topic is related to your service or product
- They should think of you as the reference
- They should introduce you

The best way to increase the likelihood that these three steps happen is to continuously communicate with your clients and give extra value to improve your relationship and expert status (they think of you as the reference). Trigger their minds with questions such as, "If you know someone who might be interested in—," so that they actually will look for situations where they can help people (they have to notice that the conversation is about that topic). And finally give them tools to increase the likelihood of introducing you. These can be discounts, special VIP treatment, and extra bonuses—not for them but to give to their friends so they raise their social status!

Besides the free referral model, there is indeed a paid one that you should not neglect: affiliate or JV partners. But this is totally different and here you really pay people a commission to sell your products. But they'll do it as professionals. They will act as an external sales and marketing division and have to inform their customers that they get compensated for every sale. It is crucial to recruit these partners. They will help you to gain the speed that is needed to grow your business before someone else copies it and overtakes you. How you can further improve your speed will be the topic of the next chapter.

CHAPTER 11

Automate Your Business

"A man is rich in proportion to the number of things he can afford to let alone"

Henry David Thoreau, Naturalist

Many businesses often face plateaus of growth. This growth depends usually on the available resources and time. These resources can be spent either to operate or to contact more customers. They then have to decide to employ more people, more sales reps with the risk that they might not grow the bottom line. In the past one solution was to spend more on below the line marketing like direct mailings. It was indeed a way to scale in a cheaper way. Then came the Internet and now online marketing is even cheaper. We have seen throughout this book, online marketing is not only setting up a website or mass mailing to all of your prospects, there is a lot more. You should now have a fair understanding of what to do. The complexity however is that each prospect has a different nurturing need and different timeframe.

And most of the follow up we wish to do often keeps staying on the wish list. There needs to be an automated process behind it. A system that follows up with each customer or prospect based on his or her needs and at the desired speed. A system that not only allows doing this automatically without increasing the sales force or marketing department but also helps the sales reps to be more efficient and effective by flagging the "hot leads" that are already educated and prepared for a visit. In some cases it even allows to completely bypass physical sales reps and automate the entire funnel from finding the prospects converting him, upselling him and keeping him in a systematic way.

Marketing Automation is integrating all the bits and pieces that might exist in the sales and marketing department, into one holistic automated software. It allows looking at a list of potential customers and prioritizing them based on the likelihood to buy. The great mistake I see many companies make is that they concentrate all efforts on choosing technology and then automate their existing process. But this is not the way you should automate your business.

The automation also does not end once someone becomes a customer. Often the real value creation comes from the retention of your clients and improving that customer relationship over time. This means more than sending a monthly newsletter, but personalized content based on their behavior, just like a real friend relationship. We are not used to automatic and instant communication. We have been used to making sales happen. You called the prospects or visited more customers when you needed more sales. The automation will replace the individual events and make it evergreen. We will only broadcast to a segment when it's relevant information for all of them. Mostly this will happen when the information is linked to a certain period of the year. For example you might want to do a Halloween promotion or a Valentine's communication.

Once you have designed the roadmap, you need to feed it with content. This is often the biggest challenge we see with our clients. So much content is being produced every day that prospects and customers are filtering all this information and only read the information that really interests them. Content where we brag about how good we are or in which we try to only sell stuff in it will definitely not pass the gateway. So we have to do a very good job in giving the customer or prospect what he wants; answering his main problems and helping him in his buying process. This is a new way of thinking about Marketing, where content is king. The content should not be created from scratch and most companies do already have a lot of content that just needs to be repurposed or repackaged. You can use speeches, videos, photos, former newsletters. And if you still need more, just curate existing topic. Good content is perhaps the most important piece and something that you cannot really automate. It's the fuel to make the whole machine work. If you want to know more on how to create content I highly recommend that you read "Epic Content Marketing" from Joe Pulizzi.

If you put all the pieces together: a clear roadmap with great content along the way integrated in a marketing automation tool you will see spectacular results with less resources. On top of that it will give you the extra insights and metrics in order to improve even further your machine.

Epilogue

"The error of youth is to believe that intelligence is a substitute for experience, while the error of age is to believe experience is a substitute for intelligence."

Lyman Bryson

As most things in life, nothing is either black or white, the same is true for marketing. Armed with the knowledge from this book you now have to design your process. There needs to be creativity involved. There are both art and science in it. To be a good artist you need to know the basics, the mechanics behind the process and how to use your gear. One of my hobbies is photography. I am not a professional but I try to take good pictures. What I learned from practicing my hobby is that you cannot be a good photographer without knowing how to use your gear and without knowing the basics of composition and luminosity. You might get a lucky shot, same with marketing. But if you want to be a pro who performs consistently, you need to understand and apply the science in your art. You need to study the theory and apply. In the beginning the shots will be average, but by applying it over and over again, only then will you make award-winning photographs on a consistent basis.

Online marketing is very similar. What you have just read is the theory, but if you do not apply it will remain fade away with time. I hope that reading this book will have brought you more clarity and given you the basics in order to start your successful marketing campaigns. But my real desire is that you apply it. One of the worst things is to know and not to take action. It might not work perfectly from the start; this is the usual way in life. If you want to master something you first have to do it poorly. Remember learning to play tennis or ride a bike? In today's world where everything changes so quickly you have to adapt accordingly. The speed of implementation is therefore more than ever critical. What works today will not work next year. Your idea or business might get copied and improved very quickly. Therefore it is important to launch your product or service as fast as possible. You should be the first in your category.

Many entrepreneurs have good ideas but procrastinate and wait until their product is near to perfect. Today this is a big mistake. You have to test it out and tweak it. As Seth Godin says "You have to ship and touch the market"[44] then you'll know whether it works. If it doesn't you learn to fail fast, and tweak. If it works you test further how to improve and then scale it into an automated process. Also think of leveraging what already exists in your market and on the web. Are there potential partners that are selling to the same market as you do? Even if you have to pay them a huge margin or give away your product completely, they will be a boost to get you running. Think out of the box and also evaluate the possibility to use your competitors as affiliates. Look at affiliate networks. Can you use them? Leverage your clients as much as possible using the techniques I explained in the previous chapter. And last but not least don't try to do everything yourself. The world is flat today and you can have access to the brightest or cheapest people around the whole world. Use sites like www.odesk.com or www.elance.com to find resources that will do things better and cheaper than you can do locally!

Whether you are a starter, have an existing business or a Fortune 500 company, if you are stuck or want some help you can go to www.bluecompass.eu or http://www.braintower.com/en/areas-of-expertise/online-marketing/ and leave your name and e-mail and I'll be happy to help or to coach you.

Thierry Moubax

---

44   Godin, Seth (2010). *Linchpin: Are You Indispensable?*

Acknowledgments

First of all I would like to thank you, reader for taking the time and effort to read my book. I hope you've enjoyed it and learned a lot from it. I feel very fortunate to be able to share with you what I have learned and experienced during my online journey.

They say that those who climb the Mountain Everest have a great sensation of fulfillment and joy when they finally reach the top of the mountain. The experience to share it with others back in the basecamp however is even better and is the ultimate satisfaction, far better than reaching the top. Sharing creations and achievements with others is usually the best part of a challenge. It's like the little toddler that after enjoying making a drawing shows his creation to his parents.

Writing this book has been like climbing the Mount Everest. The journey has been a real challenge and as with every challenge in life it has not been an easy process. There were fun parts but also difficult moments in which I really was wondering whether the effort was worth it and whether I would continue. Without the help and inspiration of many people finishing this book wouldn't have been possible.

Therefore I am very grateful to all that helped me directly or indirectly with it.

It is impossible to thank everyone therefore I already apologize that I cannot mention all of you below.

First I want to dedicate the book to my father Joseph who left us too early. He gave me this sense of curiosity and the addiction to learn and read on a continuous basis. Thank you daddy!

To my wife Felisa. For the support and love you give me every day in good and bad moments.

To Guillermo and Sofia. You are the sunshines of my life.

To my mom, Jacqueline. You are always there when I need you and you mean a lot to me.

To my sisters and the rest of the family.

My story of becoming an expert in this field began as being a student and a seeker. I therefore want to thank all my incredible teachers and Internet friends. I want to give full credit to them, because they guided me in this new world.

To Ed Dale, the founder of the 30 Day Challenge. You were my starting point in this online world and my first mentor.

To Trey Smith, The Gameacademy founder. You initiated me in the world of Apps.

To Brendon Burchard, the founder of Experts Academy. Your strategies and tactics are of immense value.

To Dean Jackson and Joe Polish. I also love Marketing as much as you do!

To all the other Internet and non Internet experts: Eben Pagan, Ryan Deiss, Perry Belcher, Dan Sullivan, Frank Kern, Jeff Johnson, Mike Koeings, Perry Marshall, Paul Colligan, Jef Walker, Andy Jenkins, James Schramko, Brian Kurtz, Andre Chaperon, Tim Ferris, Dan Kennedy, Bob Procter, Ezra Firestone, Greg Habstritt, Wyatt Woodsmall. I learned a lot from you.

I want to especially thank those who have helped me directly with the book: to Jan De Lancker, Sofie De Lancker, Anita Jovanovic, Emmanuelle Bon, Alexander Pokusay.

Last but not least I want to thank all my friends, business partners, co-workers and ex-colleagues and clients. Many have had a big impact in my life.

Naming all of you would fill too many pages, but I want to thank especially those that were directly or indirectly part of my online journey.

To Alexander Debaets, Adrien de Roubaix, Christophe Dahy, Dominique Derom, Emilio Romero, Faruk Akosman, Jean-Marie

Wodon, Kholoud Aldosari, Koen Abbeel, Laura Ibañez, Mark Peeters, Marta Belloso, Monika Thoma, Nathan Axford, Salim Barami, Sergey Efimov, Wim Focquet, Adriana Montejo, Ramon Martinez, Daniel Murray, Alexandre Centner, Bernardo Montero, Brendon Grunewald, Geert Coppens and Mehdi.

To all my friends other Pieter, Kris, Gert, Sven, Laurent, Jose Antoniò, Stephen, Grit, Flor, Myriam, Roland, Raul, Jan, Bert, José, Laura, Isabel, David, Luis and many others. I feel so lucky to have so many great relationships in my life.

Finally to those that will share this book with their friends and loved ones;
    I appreciate your support!

About the Author

Thierry Moubax is a marketing expert, consultant, and coach. He has more than twenty years of international corporate experience. He has worked in executive positions for companies such as Shell, DHL, and Securitas, in various countries.

He is also an entrepreneur and the founder of an App business –Bluecompass.eu- that makes educational apps for kids in several languages. His App business crossed the 1 million downloads within 18 months of launching it.

When he left the corporate world four years ago, his passion for technology and online marketing triggered him to master this "underground" world better. Through dozens of online courses, seminars in the United States and being part of mastermind groups, he worked his way through this "geek world" and has become an authority in the field of online marketing, both in Belgium and abroad.

Today Thierry is a partner of BrainTower, an international Marketing & Sales Consulting Company, and helps start-ups, SMEs, corporations, and governmental institutions with their online business and marketing strategies, so that they can grow their business in a more effective and efficient way. His client portfolio includes the Belgian Institute of Public Health; Belgian Post; the Belgian Railways; DHL; Moovly, an animation software start-up, IPBuilding, a technology company that creates home automation software and hardware, an educational platform; the official importer of Sebago, Aigle and Catfootwear.

He is also a frequent speaker at seminars worldwide, does in-house training sessions, and teaches beginners how to make their first dollar online.

Thierry holds a master's degree in commercial engineering from the Catholic University of Leuven, Belgium.

He is also a Certified Partner for Infusionsoft.

If you want some help or want to get in contact with him please go to **www.bluecompass.eu** or **www.braintower.com/en**.

Or you can email him at **moubax@bluecompass.eu**.

You can also follow him on **www.facebook.com/moubax**

DO ME A FAVOR?

If you have enjoyed this book and think it is worth it post your thoughts on my Amazon.com page and help share the message.

If you want more, go to
www.bluecompass.eu
and get some complementary free stuff.